Israel, Palestine, and the Quest for Middle East Peace

Dennis J. Deeb II

University Press of America,® Inc.
Lanham • Boulder • New York • Toronto • Plymouth, UK

Copyright © 2013 by University Press of America,® Inc.
4501 Forbes Boulevard, Suite 200, Lanham, Maryland 20706
UPA Aquisitions Department (301) 459-3366

10 Thornbury Road, Plymouth PL6 7PP, United Kingdom

All rights reserved

British Library Cataloguing in Publication Information Available

Library of Congress Control Number: 2013932418
ISBN: 978-0-7618-6099-0 (paperback : alk. paper)—ISBN: 978-0-7618-6100-3 (electronic)

Dedicated to my niece, Lolly, and my nephew, J.J. May the world that they embark upon be a more peaceful one for them and for all of the next generation.

Contents

Acknowledgments	vii
Introduction	ix
1 Palestine under Ottoman Rule	1
2 The Origins of Conflict: Israel & the Palestinians	5
3 From Algiers to Oslo	11
4 Failure at Camp David and the Collapse of Oslo	19
5 Resurrecting the Oslo Accords: The Mitchell Report	25
6 Israel's Policy of Unilateral Disengagement	35
7 Palestinian Elections and New Tensions with Israel	39
8 The Road Map to Peace and Alternatives to Oslo	49
9 Why Oslo Failed: A Historiography	55
10 The U.S. as Mediator: Is Peace Possible?	67
Conclusion	77
Appendix 1: United Nations Resolutions 242 and 338 upon Which the Oslo Agreements Were Based	81
Appendix 2: The Oslo Agreement: Declaration of Principles on Interim Self-Government Arrangements: September 13, 1993	85
Bibliography	97
Index	99
About the Author	103

Acknowledgments

I would like to thank the following individuals for their assistance and support in critiquing and helping me to critique this work: *De an Bergeron* and *Nidal Haschem*.

Introduction

The year 2012 seems to offer little hope for a lasting peace in the Middle East and a settlement of the Israeli-Palestinian conflict. For more than sixty years, Israelis and Palestinians have strived to make significant gains and accomplishments at the expense of the other side. The primary purpose of the Oslo Peace Accords, signed by Israeli and Palestinian leaders in 1993, was to establish a process that would enable the Israelis and Palestinians to reach a Permanent Status Agreement based on peace, co-existence, and mutual recognition. The Oslo Accords allowed for all of the disputed issues between Israelis and Palestinians to be brought to the table, negotiated, and ultimately resolved. But both sides failed to see the Accords to their conclusion and reach a final status agreement.

The age old conflict between the Israelis and the Palestinians is really a tragic tale of two peoples. Countless Israelis and Palestinian Arabs have lost their lives in conflict for causes they truly believed in. Many more have been killed or seriously injured because they just happened to be in the wrong place at the wrong time. I believe that a lasting peace agreement between both sides that guarantees the security of Israel, while acknowledging the right of self-determination and statehood by the Palestinians, is in the best interests of both sides as well as in the interests of the world community.

The chapters that follow are intended to educate readers as to events surrounding the Israeli-Palestinian conflict, the failures of the Oslo Peace Accords to provide a lasting settlement, the actions and policies followed by the Israeli Government and Palestinian Authority since 1993, and the issues that both sides need to resolve to reach a meaningful and lasting peace settlement. This book is intended largely as a follow-up to my 2003 book, *The Collapse of Middle East Peace: The Rise and Fall of the Oslo Peace Accords*. Much has happened since my first book was published, including the aftermath of the September 11th Terror attacks on the United States as well as the U.S.-led wars in Iraq and Afghanistan. In addition, both the Israelis and the Palestinians have witnessed significant changes in leadership and important developments since that time.

This book aims to provide both a historical narrative of the events surrounding the Israeli-Palestinian conflict and a historiography exploring the failures of the Oslo Peace Accords to achieve the end result of a final settlement between the Israelis and the Palestinians. Finally, this book explores the issues of contention that must be resolved between the parties to reach a lasting settlement. For a much more in-depth history and analysis of the Israeli-Arab conflicts, I would suggest reading Thomas L. Friedman's best-selling book, *From Beirut To Jerusalem*. Friedman's book outlines the issues surrounding the whole Arab-Israeli conflict in a way that everyone can understand.

I hope that this publication will inspire both Israelis and Palestinians to work to achieve a lasting peace settlement, rooted in the Oslo Peace Accords, and based on mutual recognition, respect, autonomy, and the peaceful co-existence of both Israel and an independent Palestinian State. The bulk of the writing contained in this work was written between 2007 and 2012. I have included some background information from my previous book, which is still relevant in considering the Israeli-Palestinian conflict. In the pages that follow, I have attempted to include up-to-date information on the Israeli-Palestinian conflict through July 2012. To achieve peace, both sides will have to compromise. Both sides will have to give. Let us hope that both sides will seize the opportunity to achieve a lasting peace.

Chapter One

Palestine under Ottoman Rule

The Ottoman Empire exercised control over much of the Middle East beginning in the 14th century and lasting until the end of World War I. The Ottomans were a Turkish tribe named after their Chief Osman Bey (Osman I), who assumed power in 1284. Beginning in 1299-1300, the Ottomans settled and gained control over most of the Middle East, northern Africa, and parts of Southern Europe, including Albania, Bulgaria, Greece, Hungary, Romania, and Yugoslavia. In 1453, the Ottomans seized control over the former Byzantine capital of Constantinople, and shortly afterwards, renamed the city Istanbul. This conquest marked the end of the Eastern Roman Empire. Istanbul, which was a historically important trading city, remained the capital of the Ottoman capital until the Empire's ultimate collapse in 1923.

The Ottomans incorporated Palestine into their Empire in 1516. The population of Palestine in 1850 is estimated to have had about 350,000 residents, roughly 85% were Muslims, 11% were Christians, and 4% Jews.[1] In 1914 Palestine had an estimated population of 657,000 Muslim Arabs, 81,000 Christian Arabs, and 59,000 Jews.[2]

Ottoman society was organized into millets, or nations, according to religion. The millets were administrative units based on religious identity. Each millet maintained its own internal laws and was afforded nominal authority. The Ottomans used this millet system of government to control the regions of its Empire. Under the millet system, each community was governed separately and followed their own rules, but the entire Empire was under the rule of the Ottoman Sultan, who was similar to a European monarch. During the height of the Empire, it contained a total population of approximately 40 million people. The Ottomans were very advanced culturally and militarily and many European nations during the Renaissance feared the expansion of Ottoman rule in Europe.

Under the Ottomans, Palestine continued to be linked administratively to Damascus until 1830. Later it was placed under Sidon, until it was once again placed under Damascus until 1888. Palestine was finally divided into the districts of Nabulus and Acre, both of which were linked with the then province of Beirut and the autonomous district of Jerusalem, which dealt directly with Istanbul.

The Ottoman state system, and later empire, was built on the foundation of an Islamic theocracy. The sultan stood at the top of the political system and Islam stood as the supreme ideology, which served to justify the sultan's rules and ambitions. Islam defined the sultan's role as sovereign and it defined his authority over both society and the state. The sultan was responsible only to God and this law was contained in the Sharia (Islamic Holy Law). The sultan was the chief executive of Islam and served as absolute ruler of the state. The sultan exercised absolute military authority and held title to all of the empire's lands.

The Holy Law of Islam holds that there is no human legislative authority. All law comes from God, not man. According to the teachings of the Sharia, God is the only source of law and sovereignty. The Sharia was promulgated by legislation and authorized by interpretation. The ulema, Islamic scholars, were authorized to interpret Sharia through their understanding of Islam.

The sultan's absolute power was intended to achieve specific objectives. These encompassed four state goals: 1) To further conquest and territorial expansion; 2) To promote and spread Islam; 3) The exploitation of the Empire's wealth; and 4) The preservation of domestic order and stability. In concentrating on these four goals, most of the sultans seemed to hold a Laissez-Faire attitude towards other things. As a result, there has been an emergence of growing literature that has confused the theocratic state's indifference towards non-Muslims with benevolence. Although non-Muslims were left to themselves when it came to many things, this practice of group autonomy was neither a restriction overreach, nor did it reflect multicultural tolerance of non-Muslim peoples. The sultan could rely on an appointed state bureaucracy to ensure the loyalty of his subjects. The sultan, however, reserved the right to interfere in any aspect of society where state interests were served. The Ottoman Empire extended certain privileges to Christians and Jews who supplied service, tax revenue, and loyalty to the Empire.

Two major social classes formed the Ottoman landscape and each had its own functions and privileges. These two classes were the Osmanli, or ruling class, and the Rayah, or subject class. The subject class was subordinate to the ruling class, but were allowed to enjoy certain privileges in return for serving the state. Thus, they were "tolerated," but not necessarily accepted.

The chief function of the ruling class, or Osmanli, was to govern and defend the empire. The needs and interests of the Rayah, or subject class, were generally ignored, provided that the Rayah satisfied their obligations to the state. The Rayah needed to produce wealth and resources, which included taxes and soldiers, to serve state interests.

Religion, residence, and occupation were most important in determining status and identity in Ottoman society. There were two chief categories of residence: 1) Settled populations; and 2) Unsettled populations. Each group had its own privileges and obligations.

The settled populations were people living within the Empire's cities and towns. They were free from most taxation and forced labor requirements. Those who wanted to move to cities had to pay a special tax and prove that they were able. City residents were also registered with local governments.

The unsettled populations were nomadic peoples who traveled from place-to-place. They were thus exempt from many of the Ottoman regulations. The Ottomans often dealt with these nomadic populations as tribes. Hunting, farming, and trading were the chief means of survival for these peoples. Meat, cheese, butter, and yogurt were produced by the nomads and a portion of these were collected for taxes by the Ottoman authorities.

Religion was the most important determinant of status. The Ottoman Empire was an Islamic war machine whose goal was constant expansion. The lives of ordinary subject people (Rayah) existed and were tolerated in order to satisfy the needs of the Ottoman system. The Christians, as the Empire's largest group of subject peoples, were first impacted by this reality. Their agriculture was designed to sustain the needs of a feudal military caste. Taxes collected financed the sultan's wars and Christian children were confiscated for military service. The non-Muslim inhabitants were regarded as a resource to be tapped for man-power and material in pursuit of Islamic expansion. Thus, the customs, religious beliefs, culture, etc. of Christians were of no interest to the sultanate so long as they provided resources to the state and did not challenge the state's absolute authority. Many Christians were marginalized while others benefited from "Ottoman tolerance."

Another determination of status was occupation. A majority of the subject population consisted of farmers, craftsmen, and merchants. Those who worked the land and engaged in the crafts worked in the most tightly regulated part of the Ottoman State since they produced a bulk of the resources to sustain Ottoman growth.

The Ottoman Empire began to experience a long decline due to ineffective leadership starting in the 18th century. During the 19th century, wars broke out in both Greece and Egypt. Both nations wanted independence from the Empire and the Empire itself grew even weaker during this time. When World War I broke out, the Ottoman leadership sided with Germany and Austria against England and France. World War I led to the ultimate collapse of the Ottoman Empire as forces of nationalism swept through much of the regions under its control. The Ottoman Empire eventually fell in 1923, shortly after World War I itself ended.

The collapse of the Ottoman Empire marked the end of an era. The modern Middle East emerged following the collapse of the Ottoman Empire as European powers scrambled for territory during the 1920's.[3] Thus, the collapse of the Ottoman Empire paved the way for the creation of the state of Israel, following World War II in 1948.

The Ottoman Empire had administered the Middle East from the Late Middle Ages until the Sultanate was dismantled after World War I. Following the victory of France and Britain in World War I, those countries sought to carve up the Middle East amongst each other following the demise of the Ottoman Empire.

NOTES

1. Justin McCarthy. *The Population of Palestine: Population History and Statistics of the Late Ottoman Period and the Mandate* (New York: Columbia University Press, 1990).
2. Justin McCarthy, "Palestine's Population During The Ottoman And The British Mandate Periods." Posted September 8, 2001. http://www.palestineremembered.com/Acre/Palestine-Remembered/Story559.html
3. Richard Haas, "The New Middle East." *Foreign Affairs* (November/December 2006): 3.

Chapter Two

The Origins of Conflict

Israel & the Palestinians

Following World War I, nationalist movements sprang up across the Middle East and France and Britain began to relinquish control over the region. These movements grew stronger during the 1930's and 1940's and borders were artificially drawn up shortly after the end of World War II. *New York Times* correspondent Sam Roberts correctly observes, "In drawing the boundaries of what would become today's Iraq, Jordan, Israel, Syria, and Lebanon, they paid little attention to the ancient tribal, ethnic, and religious differences that are at the root of much of the bloodshed in the region 90 years later."[1]

Colonel E.M. House, a close advisor to U.S. President Woodrow Wilson, had pessimistically predicted that the boundaries drawn up in the Middle East by the European powers were "making a breeding place for future war."[2]

The Palestinian Arabs owned 97% of the land in Palestine in 1917. Britain created the Palestine problem in 1917 with the release of the Balfour Declaration. The Balfour Declaration consisted of a letter written by British Foreign Secretary Arthur James Balfour to Baron Rothschild, who was a leader of Britain's Jewish community, stating that the British Government was in favor of and would support the creation of a Jewish national homeland in Palestine. Only about 56,000 Jews lived in Palestine in that year and less than 5% of the Jewish residents living in Palestine in 1917 were born in Palestine.[3]

The conflict between Palestinians and Israelis has its roots in the late nineteenth and the early twentieth century. During this time, Jewish settlers began to settle in Palestine. These Jews were driven by the nationalist sentiment of Zionism. The Zionists encouraged Jews worldwide to settle in Palestine and to help create an independent Jewish state in that region. Most of the Jews who migrated to Palestine in the 1920's were motivated, skilled, and well-organized.[4]

During the first part of the twentieth century, both Arab and Jewish settlers from Europe resided in Palestine. Thomas Friedman, a Pulitzer Prize-winning correspondent of *The New York Times*, wrote, "Most of the early Zionists either ignored the presence of the Arabs already in Palestine or assumed they could either be bought off or would eventually submit to Jewish domination."[5] As we know, the problem never disappeared but tensions only escalated in the years that followed.

David Ben-Gurion, Israel's first Prime Minister, stated in 1937, "The boundaries of Zionist aspirations are the concern of the Jewish people, and no external factor will be able to limit them."[6] Ben-Gurion later told the Zionist Executive Committee that "after the formation of a large army…we will abolish partition and expand to the whole of Palestine."[7] It should be noted that many Israelis and Jews reject this policy of Zionist expansionism, but we can see that the belief that Zionism as a political philosophy is racist certainly is reinforced by one of the movement's early leaders. The United Nations equated the philosophy of Zionism with racism early on.

At the end of World War II, tensions and fighting between Jewish settlers and Palestinian Arabs increased drastically. It was during this time that the Zionist movement declared its intentions of obtaining a dominant Jewish state in Palestine. In addition, after 1945, the Jewish underground, which consisted of a small minority of Jewish settlers, increased its campaign to oust British peacekeepers from Palestine. The Jewish underground charged that the British had Arab sympathies. In order to achieve their objective, the Jewish underground initiated a series of terrorist attacks against the British.[8] Shortly afterwards, the British began to make plans to withdraw from the region, removing themselves from the political struggle for control.

In the fall of 1947, Great Britain, which had tried to work out an agreement between the Palestinian Arabs and the Jewish settlers, handed the problem over to the United Nations. On November 29, 1947, the General Assembly of the United Nations voted thirty-three to thirteen to divide Palestine into two states - one Jewish and one Arab. The Jewish state would consist of the coastal plain between Tel Aviv and Haifa, northern Galilee, and the Negev Desert. The Palestinian Arab state would include the West Bank of the Jordan, the Gaza District, Jaffa, and the Arab regions of Galilee. Jerusalem, which was held most sacred by Jews, Muslims, and Christians was to be internationalized and placed under the trusteeship of the United Nations.

David Ben-Gurion, then leader of the Zionist Jewish movement, accepted this United Nations proposal however the Palestinian Arabs and surrounding Arab countries completely rejected the proposal. Soon afterwards, the British peacekeepers, who had been present in Palestine since the end of World War I, announced their intention to leave the area by May 15, 1947.

On May 14, 1947, the Provisional State Council of Tel Aviv declared independence and the creation of a Jewish state in Palestine. Both the United States and the Soviet Union recognized Israel the same day it declared its independence. As a result, Israel's Arab neighbors stepped up their efforts to drive the Jews out of Palestine. The following day, military forces from Transjordan [now Jordan], Egypt, Lebanon, Syria, Saudi Arabia, and Iraq joined Palestinian guerillas in declaring war on the Jewish state. This constituted the first Arab-Israeli War and became Israel's War for Independence.

The Arab nations and the Palestinians were unsuccessful in preventing Israel from becoming an independent Jewish state. The Israelis defeated their Arab invaders and seized control of some Palestinian Arab territories as well. Following this defeat, Jordan annexed the West Bank and Egypt seized the Gaza District. Egypt and Jordan both refused to permit the Palestinian Arabs to form their own nation in these territories. A United Nations truce was reached which defined borders and frontiers for Israel which remained unaltered until the 1967 war.

Following the War for Israeli Independence, all Palestinians were granted full citizenship in Jordan. Soon afterwards, several other Arab countries granted partial or limited citizenship to Palestinians.

The new Jewish state came to occupy seventy-seven percent of the territory in Palestine. This resulted in the migration and expulsion of more than half of the Palestinian Arab population. Since the West Bank and Gaza Strip, which was reserved for the Palestinian Arabs, was taken over by Egypt and Jordan, the Palestinian Arab state never came into being.[9] By the end of 1949, seven hundred thousand of the approximately nine hundred thousand Palestinian Arabs had fled their native Palestine as a result of terrorist attacks by the Jewish underground. The number of Jews in Palestine totaled about fifty thousand in 1917. By 1948, the Jewish population had increased to six hundred fifty thousand as a result of migration.

Throughout the 1950's tensions between Egypt and Israel increased dramatically. Egypt's President Gamel Abdel Nasser nationalized the Suez Canal which resulted in an Israeli attack on Egypt in 1956 with the assistance of Britain and France. During this attack, Egypt seized additional parts of the Gaza Strip and the Sinai Peninsula however it later withdrew from Gaza and Sinai in 1957 following pressure from both the United States and the United Nations.[10]

The United Nations Security Council condemned Israel in 1951, 1953, 1955, and again in 1956 for attacking Palestinian villages under its control and for launching military attacks against surrounding Arab nations.[11]

Arab nationalism began to emerge after this 1956 war with Israel. This led to a united Arab military command that massed army troops along the borders with Israel. These actions along with Egypt's closure of the Straits of Tiran resulted in the Israeli government simultaneously attacking Egypt, Jordan, and Syria on June 5, 1967. This war lasted six days and was a momentous victory for Israel. The Israelis occupied the Gaza Strip and Sinai Peninsula from Egypt, Arab East Jerusalem and the West Bank from Jordan, and the Golan Heights from Syria. All of these occupied lands included an Arab population of approximately one and a half million people. This resulted in yet another exodus of Palestinians. On November 22, 1967, the United Nations adopted Resolution 242, which called on Israel to withdraw from the territories it had occupied in the 1967 conflict.

The war between Israel and her Arab neighbors in June 1967 forever changed the balance of power in the Middle East in favor of the former. Egyptian President Gamal Abdel Nasser publicly stated his intentions to destroy the State of Israel following the 1967 War. During this time, Israel began employing Palestinian refugees in the West Bank and Gaza Strip. Many of these Palestinian workers labored for low wages and were afforded minimal benefits. This is still the case today in Israel. Israeli-occupation of the West Bank pushed more than four hundred thousand more Palestinians into neighboring Jordan.[12]

The Arab states created the Palestine Liberation Organization [PLO] in 1964. At first, its leaders were viewed as puppets of Egypt and Egyptian President Nasser. During this time, the PLO was extremist and largely disorganized. It received little recognition or backing from the Palestinian people. In 1969, a successful engineer, Yasir Arafat, became Chairman of the PLO. He enjoyed popular and widespread support from the Palestinian people and sought international recognition for the PLO.

Yasir Arafat was born in 1929 as one of seven children of a wealthy Palestinian merchant. Investigative reporter Thomas Friedman maintains that Arafat was able to keep the PLO independent and strong as a result of his skillful political maneuvering. Friedman writes, "Arafat did for the Palestinians what the Zionists did for the Jews: brought them from oblivion back into politics."[13]

Egypt and Syria attacked Israel on October 6, 1973 in an attempt to take back the areas lost in the 1967 war. This attack occurred on one of Israel's holiest days, Yom Kippur. For about three weeks, the Egyptian and Syrian forces seemed to be defeating the Israeli military. Military and financial assistance from the United States eventually helped Israel to fend off the Arab armies by October 24, 1973. United States Secretary of State Henry Kissinger was sent by President Richard Nixon to negotiate an agreement between Israel and Egypt in the Sinai and Israel and Syria in the Golan Heights in 1974.[14]

Palestinian guerilla forces had been operating out of Lebanon since 1978. These guerillas engaged in a series of attacks against Israel from the Lebanese border. On June 6, 1982, the Israeli military invaded Lebanon in an organized effort to destroy the PLO. Eight days later, both Syrian troops and the PLO forces were surrounded. They were forced to retreat to Syria in August. Soon afterwards, a cease-fire agreement was arranged and the PLO withdrew from Beirut and fled to neighboring Arab countries in exchange for security guarantees for thousands of Palestinian refugees left behind.[15] Thousands of Lebanese and Palestinian civilians were killed or injured following the 1982 conflict with Israel. These will be discussed further later on. By February 1985, the Israeli army withdrew from Lebanon however, it maintained a 'security zone' on the border. Border skirmishes continued between Palestinian guerillas and Israeli military forces throughout the 1980's.

Since 1967, Palestinians living in the Occupied Territories of the West Bank and Gaza Strip have been living under military authority. They are prohibited from voting, joining a labor unit, organizing politically, can be detained without formal charges, may be deported, and can have their property seized for Israeli settlements.[16]

An organized Palestinian revolt against Israeli-occupation, the Palestinian Intifada [uprising], began following an Israeli vehicle crash that killed four Palestinians on December 8, 1987. It first began in the Jebalya refugee camp in the Gaza Strip to protest living conditions and treatment by Israeli authorities.[17] The Intifada lasted from 1987 to 1993 in the Israeli-occupied territories of the West Bank and Gaza Strip. The Uprising captured the attention and sympathy of much of the world community as hundreds of thousands of displaced Palestinian refugees took to the streets to protest what they viewed were deplorable living conditions and gross human rights violations at the hands of Israeli government authorities. The Intifada led to daily strikes and demonstrations by Palestinians, mostly youths, throwing stones and protesting physically in order to attract world attention to the Palestinian cause for self-determination.

NOTES

1. Sam Roberts, "How The Middle East Got That Way," *The New York Times Upfront*, January 15, 2007, p. 25.
2. Ibid.
3. Fadwa El Guindi, "The Palestinian Case Against Israel," *The Free American*, January 2003.
4. Tim Llewellyn, "The Birth of Israel," *BBC Online Network*, 20 April 1998. http://news6.thdo.bbc.co.uk?hi/english/israel_at_50/history/newsid_78000/78601.stm: 1.
5. Thomas L. Friedman. *From Beirut To Jerusalem* (New York: Farrar Straus Giroux, 1989), 14.
6. Rachelle Marshall. "Obama's Patience With Israel Finally Cracks," *The Washington Report on Middle East Affairs*, May/June 2010, 7.
7. Ibid.
8. Llewellyn, "The Birth of Israel," 2.

9. United Nations, *History of the Palestinian Problem: Question of Palestine*. http://www.un.org/Depts/dpa/ngo/history.html: 1-3.

10. "Arab Israeli Wars History Text." http://members.nbci.com/_xmcm/palestine99/wartext.htm: 1-6.

11. Abdullah Frangi, "Palestinians Have A Right To A Homeland In Israel," in *The Middle East: Opposing Viewpoints*, ed. Janelle Rohr (St. Paul, Minnesota: Greenhaven Press, 1988), 137.

12. Tim Llewellyn, "Israel and the PLO," *BBC Online Network*, 20 April 1998. http://news6thdo.bbc.co./uk/hi/English/events/israel_at_50/history/newsid_78000/78655.stm: 1.

13. Friedman, *From Beirut To Jerusalem*, 108.

14. "Arab Israeli Wars History Text," 1-6.

15. United Nations, *History of the Palestinian Problem: Question of Palestine*, 2.

16. Ronald Stockton, "Teaching the Israeli-Palestinian Conflict," (Dearborn, Michigan: November 1993). http://www.umich.edu/~iinet/cmenas/StudyUnits/israeli-palestinianconflict/index.html.

17. Mark Perry, *A Fire In Zion: The Israeli-Palestinian Search For Peace* (New York: William Marrow and Company, 1994), 11.

Chapter Three

From Algiers to Oslo

In a June 1988 summit in Algiers, Arab nations officially recognized the Palestine Liberation Organization [PLO] as the sole representative of the Palestinian people and Jordan's King Hussein renounced all claim to the West Bank which paved the way for the Palestinians to create their own independent state there if they could achieve a peace settlement with Israel.

In November 1988, the Palestine National Council, led by Yasir Arafat and the PLO, voted to accept the United Nations Resolutions 181 and 242 to accept the legitimacy of both a Jewish and Palestinian State. Resolution 181 acknowledged the right of Israel to exist as a sovereign nation and proposed that the City of Jerusalem be internationalized while Resolution 242 called on Israel to withdraw to its pre-1967 borders. In addition, the PLO formally renounced terrorism and endorsed negotiations to obtain a lasting settlement with the government of Israel.

Although many Palestinian citizens, including some PLO leaders, had said for years that they accepted a 'two-state' solution, encompassing both a Jewish and Palestinian state, to the Israeli-Palestinian conflict, it was not until 1988 that an official PLO declaration was made.[1] Following this declaration, the United States joined the rest of the world community in recognizing the PLO and engaging in dialogue with its leaders, including Arafat.

The Intifada, or resistance, began on the 70th anniversary of the British military conquest of Palestine. This First Intifada encompassed an uprising by Palestinian residents of the Occupied West Bank and Gaza Strip. This uprising, which initially encompassed a series of non-violent civil disobedience and resistance to Israeli occupation, started in December 1987 and lasted until the signing of the Oslo Peace Accords in 1993. These demonstrators claimed that they had suffered long enough from the oppressive and inhumane treatment imposed on them for twenty-one years by Israeli government authorities.² The Palestinians living in the Israeli-occupied West Bank and Gaza Strip were clearly being treated as second class citizens.

Just before the beginning of the Intifada, the Israeli government had established an advanced computerized databank in the West Bank and Gaza Strip for the stated purpose of keeping track of every Palestinian's property, family history, political leanings, job occupation, licensing, consumption, and participation in illegal activities. West Bank expert Meron Benvenisti referred to this computerized databank as "the ultimate instrument of population control."³

When it began, the Intifada encompassed a completely unarmed Palestinian population that consisted of a mere one-third the size of the Israeli Jewish population. The Intifada caught the Israeli government by surprise.⁴ This First Intifada marked the first time that Palestinian population united as a nation to oppose Israeli occupation.

After the beginning of the Intifada, several Palestinians refused to pay taxes to the Israeli government. In response, the Israeli authorities announced that they were going to require all Palestinians to carry a new identity card in order to travel or hold a job. A condition for obtaining the new card was to pay all back taxes and to prove that no family member was wanted by the Israeli military. These actions made life even more difficult for countless Palestinians struggling to survive Israeli-occupation.

Seventy-five percent of the Palestinian population in the West Bank is under twenty-eight years old.⁵ The Intifada ultimately served to empower Palestinian laborers, workers, and Palestinian youth.⁶ United Nations correspondent Phyllis Bennett observed, "Israeli efforts to suppress the Intifada have included widespread collective punishment aimed at the entire population."⁷ Collective punishment has been outlawed by the 1949 Geneva Convention. Collective punishment serves only to foster more hatred and violence. Thomas Friedman summarized the underlying goal of many Palestinians in the Intifada. He writes, "The Palestinians must make themselves so indigestible to Israelis that they want to disgorge them into their own state, while at the same time reassuring the Israelis that they can disgorge them without committing suicide."⁸

At the November 15, 1988 meeting of the Palestine National Council in Algiers, Algeria, hundreds of Palestinian refugees and hundreds more newspaper reporters and media analysts gathered to hear the declaration of independence of the new nation of Palestine by PLO Chairman Yasir Arafat.

During the first four years of the Intifada, more than one hundred hand grenade attacks and six hundred assaults with guns or explosives were reported by the government of Israel. The violence was directed at Israeli soldiers and Palestinians alike.⁹

Rioting and clashes between Palestinian protestors and Israeli troops continued in the early 1990's. The violence encompassed a continuation of stone-throwing and the use of homemade explosive devices on behalf of the Palestinians. Israeli troops utilized tear gas, rubber bullets, and home demolition in attempting to quell popular resistance.[10]

Israel worked to promote Hamas to counter the influence of the more secular Fatah throughout the 1980's. As a fundamentalist Islamic organization, Hamas was a staunch opponent of secular Palestinian nationalism throughout the 1970's and 1980's. Hamas often fought with the PLO and Fatah, the political and military wing of the Palestinian liberation movement whose goal was to liberate Palestine from Israeli control. Israel initially supported and encouraged Hamas in order to fraction the national ambitions of the Palestinians.[11]

The Arab nations have to share some blame for the plight of the Palestinian people. While controlling the West Bank and Gaza Strip, Jordan and Egypt refused to permit the formation of an independent Palestinian state.

In 1991, following the Persian Gulf War, peace talks began at Madrid between Israelis, Palestinians, Lebanese, Syrians, and Jordanians. Between November 3 and November 9, 1991, the first round of bilateral discussions between Israeli and Palestinian authorities was held in Madrid, Spain. A second round of negotiations between Israeli and Palestinian authorities was held in Washington, D.C. from December 10-18, 1991. Little was accomplished in these discussions. Additional talks were held between Israelis and Palestinians from January 13-16, 1992 in Washington, D.C. Israel's Likud Party Prime Minister Yitzhak Shamir and his delegation presided over these talks. Israel's Likud Party was opposed and still is opposed to the creation of an independent Palestinian state co-existing alongside Israel.

On June 23, 1992, Yitzhak Rabin was elected Prime Minister. Rabin was a leader of the Israel's moderate Labor Party, which favored direct negotiations with the Palestinians resulting in a peace settlement. Rabin's election would change the course of history. Rabin envisioned a lasting peace settlement between Israelis and Palestinians. Rabin was a true visionary and man of peace who translated words and ideas into positive action.

Yitzhak Rabin served as Israel's Prime Minister from 1974 to 1977 and again from 1992 to 1995. His latter term concerns us here. In 1992, Rabin defeated Shimon Peres for leadership of Israel's Labor Party and then as Prime Minister however, Rabin later appointed Peres as his Foreign Minister. Rabin was born on March 3, 1922 to Roza and Nehemya Rabin. While in high school, Rabin joined the Palmach part of the Israeli army to fight for Israeli independence from Britain.[12]

Rabin campaigned for and was elected on a platform of peace that included coming to a swift agreement on Palestinian autonomy. Rabin did not intend to settle the final status of the territories however, he would begin the long process of resolving the century-old dispute between Palestinians and Israelis. Rabin's policies and goals from 1992 to 1995 included withdrawing most of Israeli military forces from Lebanon, signing a peace accord with Jordan, and engaging in formal dialogue with the PLO.[13]

Rabin signed the Oslo Peace Agreement with PLO Leader Yasir Arafat on September 13, 1993 in Washington, D.C. The agreement was originally negotiated at Oslo, Norway. In signing the agreement, Rabin remarked, "enough of the blood and tears."[14] The Oslo Peace Accords provided for mutual recognition between Israel and the PLO and for limited self-rule for the Palestinians in the Palestinian territories of Jericho and Gaza. The Agreement also stated that the Israeli government acknowledged the PLO as the sole Palestinian Authority, the legitimate representative of the Palestinian people. In return, the PLO promised to crack down on terrorism and acknowledged the existence of the State of Israel and the right of that nation to exist in peace and security. At that time, the Agreement was viewed by the Palestinians and most of the world community as an intermediate first step toward the creation of an independent Palestinian State.

The Declaration of Principles of the Interim Self-Government Agreement, which was incorporated into the Oslo Agreement, stated that the Israeli Government and the PLO team acknowledged that their peoples must "strive to live in peaceful coexistence and mutual dignity and security and achieve a just, lasting, and comprehensive peace settlement and historic reconciliation through the agreed political process."[15] The Oslo Accords established the aim of negotiations and a framework for an interim period. It also established a time frame for elections in the Palestinian areas of the West Bank and Gaza Strip, economic collaboration, withdrawal of Israeli troops from the Jericho and Gaza Strip areas, and security guarantees for Israel.[16]

The Oslo Peace Accords of 1993 specified the following arrangements:

1. A Palestinian Government
2. A Palestine Council with free elections
3. Voting rights for Palestinians
4. Limits on Palestine Council Authority
5. Israeli troop withdrawal from the West Bank and Gaza Strip
6. The creation of a strong Palestinian police force
7. A 5-year transition period for provision implementation
8. Negotiations based on United Nations Resolutions 242 and 338 leading to their implementation
9. Future Discussions and settlement on Palestinian refugees
10. Future Talks regarding the status of Jerusalem.[17]

U.N. Resolution 242 passed on November 22, 1967, called on Israel to withdraw to its pre-1967 borders and for neighboring Arab states to acknowledge Israel's sovereignty. Resolution 338, passed on October 22, 1973, called on

Israel and its Arab neighbors to implement Resolution 242 and begin negotiations aimed at establishing a permanent peace settlement in the region.

The Intifada Uprising officially ended in 1993 following the signing of the Oslo Peace Accords. During the Intifada Israeli forces had killed approximately 1,100 Palestinians and Palestinian militants had killed 164 Israelis. In promoting the Oslo Peace Accords, Rabin wrote, "Wars have their victors and their vanquished, but everyone is a victor in peace."[18] Journalist Jonathan Parker wrote, "Mr. Rabin was elected Prime Minister in 1992 and in three years came closer to peace than anyone else could have in 47 years."[19]

In May 1994, another follow-up agreement, known as the Cairo Accords, was signed by Israel and the PLO in Cairo, Egypt. This agreement provided for:

1. A scheduled withdrawal of Israeli military forces from Gaza and Jericho
2. The transfer of limited governance to the Palestinian Authority
3. A structure and composition of the Palestinian Authority
4. The establishment of legislative powers and responsibilities of the Palestinian Authority
5. An arrangement for security and public order in Palestinian areas
6. The formal creation of a Palestinian police force
7. Safe passage between the Gaza Strip and Jericho for Palestinians
8. Diplomatic relations between Israel and the Palestinian Authority
9. A liaison and cooperation between Egypt and Jordan
10. Settlement of disputes and prevention of hostile acts between the parties
11. Confidence building measures and a temporary international presence in Gaza and Jericho
12. An acknowledgement of rights, liabilities, and obligations of both parties.[20]

Under this agreement, a twenty-four member Palestinian National Authority, appointed by the PLO and headed by Yasir Arafat, would govern the region, make its laws, and would be in charge of its economic policies. However, the Israelis retained most of the security authority and were responsible for the frontier areas and buffer zones around Israeli settlements. This agreement was seen as another step in the movement toward complete Palestinian self-rule of this area and the whole West Bank. Additional agreements providing for a transfer of control to the Palestinians of other West Bank towns and the complete Gaza Strip were finalized in 1994 and 1995. These were all based upon the Oslo Accords. Under the terms of the Oslo Accords, the Palestinian Authority was obligated to refrain from incitement against Israel and to take measures to prevent others from engaging in it.

As explained earlier, the Oslo Peace Accords provided for mutual recognition between the State of Israel and the Palestine Liberation Organization [PLO] and for limited self-rule for the Palestinians in the Palestinian territories of Jericho in the West Bank and the Gaza Strip. The Agreement also provided for the Israeli government to acknowledge the PLO as the sole Palestinian Authority, the legitimate representative of the Palestinian people. In return, the PLO promised to crack down on terrorism and acknowledged the existence of the State of Israel and the right of that nation to exist in peace and security. At that time, the Agreement was viewed as an intermediate first step toward the creation of an independent Palestinian state. The Oslo Accords allowed for all of the disputed issues between the Israelis and Palestinians to be brought to the table negotiated, and ultimately resolved. The Accords provided that a final settlement would be agreed to within seven years, by September 2000.

Additional issues of contention cited in the Oslo Accords were also left to be resolved in the final status agreements. These included border parameters between Israel-Palestine, the return of Palestinian refugees, consensus on Palestinian laborers working in Israel, the removal of Israeli settlements in the Gaza Strip and West Bank, and an agreement on the status of Jerusalem.

In a letter to Rabin following the signing of the Oslo Accords, Arafat wrote that the PLO recognizes the right of the State of Israel to exist in peace and security. In addition, Arafat wrote that the PLO accepts United Nations Security Council Resolutions 242 and 338.[21] As explained earlier, these Resolutions called on Israel to withdraw to its 1967 borders. The September 9, 1993 letter read, "The PLO renounces the use of terrorism and other acts of violence and will assume responsibility over all PLO elements and personnel in order to ensure their complete compliance, prevent violations, and discipline violators."[22] Because of these historic agreements, Rabin and Arafat both would receive the Nobel Peace Prize along with future Prime Minister Shimon Peres the following year.

On September 28, 1995, Rabin participated in the signing of the Oslo B. Article XXII of the Oslo B Interim Agreement of September 28, 1995 states that Israel and the Palestinian Authority "shall seek to foster mutual understanding and tolerance and shall accordingly abstain from incitement, including hostile propaganda, against each other and, without derogating from the principle of freedom of expression, shall take legal measures to prevent such incitement by organizations, groups, or individuals within their jurisdiction."[23]

On Saturday, November 4 of the same year, following his attendance at a peace rally in Tel Aviv, Rabin was shot and killed by Igala Meir, a twenty-five-year-old Israeli extremist and law student who opposed the Oslo Accords. Following the assassination, Meir was questioned as to his motivation for killing Rabin. Meir replied, "I was opposed to the peace process."[24]

The National Alliance of Lebanese Americans, in an editorial position statement released just days after Rabin's assassination, observed that "the Israeli Prime Minister became a victim of his own peace policy when he was gunned down by a fellow Israeli."[25] The editorial asserted that prior to Rabin's election, the Israeli-Palestinian Peace talks were going nowhere. It credited Rabin with establishing a new precedent for Israel that encompassed an agenda of peace with the Palestinians and its Arab neighbors.[26] On November 22, 1995, just thirteen days following Rabin's assassination, Peres was appointed by the Israeli Knesset [parliament] as acting Prime Minister and Defense Minister. He held these two positions until the spring elections.

As mentioned earlier, Peres was the recipient of the Nobel Peace Prize in 1994, along with Arafat and Rabin, for his efforts in helping to negotiate the Oslo Peace Accords.[27] During Peres' short tenure as Prime Minister, a series of terrorist attacks and suicide bombings by Palestinians were targeted against Israel by Palestinian extremists and militants opposed to the peace process. These militants claimed that the peace process was not moving along fast enough. These actions and developments made it difficult for significant advancements to be made.[28] Peres found himself in a very difficult and complicated situation.

In early 1996, Yasir Arafat was elected President of the Palestinian-controlled territory. Arafat wasted no time in taking control and in exercising the authority awarded him under the Oslo Peace Accords. His jurisdiction encompassed designated portions of the West Bank and Gaza Strip.

NOTES

1. Ronald Stockton, "Teaching the Israeli-Palestinian Conflict," (Dearborn, Michigan: November 1993). http://www.umich.edu/~iinet/cmenas/StudyUnits/israeli-palestinianconflict/index.html.
2. Phyllis Bennis. *From Stones To Statehood: The Palestinian Uprising* (New York: Olive Branch Press, 1989), 12.
3. Thomas L. Friedman. *From Beirut To Jerusalem* (New York: Farrar Straus Giroux, 1989), 413.
4. Bennis. *From Stones To Statehood: The Palestinian Uprising*, 12-13.
5. Ibid; 44.
6. Ibid; 39.
7. Ibid; 82.
8. Friedman. *From Beirut To Jerusalem*, 421.
9. Mitchell Bard, "The Intifada," *The Jewish Student Online Research Center* (2001).
10. Columbia University Press, "Intifada," *The Columbia Electronic Encyclopedia* (2000). http://www.factmonster.com/co6/history/A0825375.
11. Brendan O'Neill, "Making Enemies: How Israel Helped To Create Hamas," *The American Conservative*, February 12, 2007, 18-19.
12. "Yitzhak Rabin." http://www.ttt.org.il/nov/rabin.htm.
13. "The Path To Peace Runs Through A History of Turmoil," *CNN.com*. http://www.cnn.com/SPECIALS/2000/mideast/story/overview/ : 1-6.
14. "Yitzhak Rabin." http://www.ttt.org.il/nov/rabin.htm.

15. "Al Mashriq - Interim Self Agreement Between Israel and the PLO,' *Israel Information Service Gopher* (September 1993). http://almashriq.hiof.no/israel/300/320/327/interim-self-gov.html: 1.

16. Ibid; 3.

17. Stockton, "Teaching the Israeli-Palestinian Conflict."

18. Yitzhak Rabin, "Israel Is Committed To Peace," in *Israel: Opposing Viewpoints* ed. Charles Cozic (San Diego: Greenhaven Press, Inc., 1994), 101.

19. Jonathan Parker, "Peace Hopes Buried." http://pages.ripco.net/~alderson/1/jpnews.htm.

20. "Agreement on the Gaza Strip and Jericho Area," *Israel Information Service Gopher*, (4 May 1994). http://almashriq.hiof.no/general/300/320/327/gaza_and_jericho_00.html.

21. "Letter From Chairman Yasir Arafat to Prime Minister Rabin," 9 September 1993. http://www.palestine-un.org/peace/p_b.html.

22. Israeli Government Printing Office. 1997. *Palestinian Incitement to Violence since Oslo: A Four-Year Compendum*: 1-16.

23. Ibid; 1.

24. Jonathan Parker, "Peace Hopes Buried." http://pages.ripco.net/~alderson/1/jpnews.htm).

25. National Alliance of Lebanese Americans, "The Passing of Yitzhak Rabin," 10 November 1995. http://www.nala.com/Editorial/RABIN.html: 1-3.

26. Ibid; 1-3.

27. "Shimon Peres: Winner of the 1994 Nobel Prize In Peace," *The Nobel Prize Internet Archive*. http://www.almaz.com/nobel/peace/1994b.html.

28. American-Israeli Cooperative Enterprise, "Shimon Peres."

Chapter Four

Failure at Camp David and the Collapse of Oslo

The period following the signing of the Oslo Peace Accords in 1993 did not have the desired result of creating a climate of trust between Israelis and Palestinians. Both sides share blame for the failures that followed. Robert Danin, who served as U.S. Deputy Assistant Secretary of State for Near Eastern Affairs from 2005 to 2008, wrote in *Foreign Affairs*, "Rather than serving to build confidence, the post-Oslo period only increased bitterness and mistrust."[1] Danin added, "Palestinians either engaged in or turned a blind eye to terrorism, and incitement to violence continued. Meanwhile, Israel continued to expand the West Bank settlements and failed to carry out previously negotiated troop redeployments from the West Bank."[2]

In May 1996, Israeli Likud Party Leader Benjamin Netanyahu, an outspoken critic of the Oslo Peace Accords, narrowly defeated Peres and was elected Israel's new Prime Minister. Netanyahu became Israel's ninth and youngest Prime Minister at thirty-seven years old. He won 50.5% of the popular vote compared to Peres' 49.5%. Netanyahu campaigned promising the eradication of terrorism and the establishment of peace. He is the author of numerous books on terrorism and Israel's security.

Benjamin Netanyahu was born on October 21, 1949. He is married and is the father of three children. He received the bulk of his education in the United States, attending high school in Philadelphia and receiving a degree from Harvard University and Massachusetts Institute of Technology.

Benjamin Netanyahu had been an outspoken critic of the peace process and gained a reputation for saying what he thought regardless of public opinion. In campaigning for Prime Minister, Netanyahu promised to undo whatever steps had been taken toward peace with the Palestinians as resembled in the Oslo Agreements. According to *CNN*, after being elected Prime

Minister, Benjamin Netanyahu "adopted an unwavering stance which did little to further the peace process."[3] Netanyahu himself wrote in a 1994 book, "If there is to be peace, it will have to mean, at long last, the recognition of Palestinian Arabs that they are in the minority in the forty miles west of the Jordan River, and they will receive no additional independent states there."[4]

Netanyahu's agenda as Prime Minister encompassed the expansion of Israeli settlements in Palestinian areas and maintaining the territory of Israel as it was with no territorial concessions to the Palestinians.[5] On October 17, 1996, Netanyahu cancelled the Labor government's freeze, instituted by Rabin and Peres, on Israeli construction in Palestinian territories while announcing plans to expand existing Israeli settlements and build new roads and industrial parks throughout the West Bank and Gaza Strip.[6] In his book, *A Durable Peace*, Netanyahu had argued that the Palestinians should settle for self-determination within Israeli jurisdiction rather than demand a completely independent state of their own.[7] Netanyahu's actions and policies increased tensions with and angered Palestinians.

Under Netanyahu's reign, violence escalated among Palestinian protesters who felt that the mission of Netanyahu's policies were intended to undermine the Oslo Peace Accords, which he continued to oppose throughout his term.

The Wye River Accords of 1998 offered a dim shade of hope for the Palestinians. The Wye River Conference between Netanyahu and Arafat was held in Maryland and was mediated by Jordan's King Hussein and President Bill Clinton. This established that the Palestinians would erase from their founding charter language that called for the destruction of the Jewish state. In return, the Netanyahu government transferred an additional thirteen percent of the West Bank to Palestinian self-rule. In addition, the deadline of September 13, 2000 was agreed on to establish a final peace agreement. This calmed some of the tensions by Palestinians but, many of the Palestinians were still very upset with the continuation of Israeli expansion settlements in the occupied territories.

On May 17, 1999, Ehud Barak, a member of the Knesset and Labor Party leader, defeated Benjamin Netanyahu and became Israel's tenth Prime Minister. Netanyahu had not only been criticized by the West for his stances with the Palestinians, he had also been attacked for his internal policies. Scandals plagued Netanyahu's government toward the latter part of his term.

Barak campaigned for Prime Minister as a centrist who supported the Peace Process with the Palestinian Authority. Ehud Barak was born in 1942 on a kibbutz that his parents helped found near the Lebanese border. Barak promised to reach a final peace settlement with the Palestinians and also hinted at a territorial compromise involving the Golan Heights with Syria in exchange for peace.[8] Unfortunately, neither of these ever came to fruition during Barak's term as Prime Minister although Barak attempted to reach a settlement with the Palestinians.

Barak had a long history of involvement in the Israeli Military and in the politics of his country. He had a distinguished military career from the time he joined the Israeli Defense Forces in 1959. In January 1982, Barak was appointed Head of the IDF Military Planning Branch and promoted to Major General. In April 1983, Barak was appointed Head of the Intelligence Branch at the IDF General Headquarters. In 1994, Barak was awarded the "Distinguished Service Medal" for his courageous military service. After serving in the Israeli military for thirty-five years in 1995, Barak retired as Army Chief of Staff and joined the Labor Party. He served briefly as Interior Minister under Rabin and as Foreign Minister under Peres. In 1996, Barak was elected to the Knesset. Later that year, he was elected Chairman of the Labor Party.

Extensive talks and negotiations between Barak and the Palestinian Authority took place during his tenure as Prime Minister however, little was accomplished with regards to a permanent peace settlement involving territorial compromise. Toward the end of President Bill Clinton's term of office in the fall of 2000, the two sides came to a complete standstill in the negotiations held at Camp David over territorial concessions, Israeli settlement expansions, and the right of return for Palestinian refugees. Talks were also stalled over the status of Jerusalem. Much was written about these events in the national and international news. The Israeli government claimed that Arafat was demanding too much and that Barak was offering the Palestinian Authority a comprehensive package that was fair and consistent with the spirit of the Oslo Accords.

The Palestinians argued that they could not accept Barak's proposal for three reasons: 1) The territory offered was scattered and the way it was configured would make a Palestinian state virtually impossible; 2) United Nations Resolution 242 called for Israel to withdraw to its 1967 borders and this was the spirit of Oslo. In their acceptance of Oslo, Palestinians accepted a two-state solution and this was a compromise of over half of the area that was originally assigned to them; and 3) The Barak offer stemmed from the continued illegal occupation, confiscation, and expropriation of Palestinian land.[9]

Other observers pointed out, "Barak's coalition was not very trustworthy... The ultraorthodox shas-Party blackmailed the government to satisfy the demands of its clientele."[10] The Shas-Party was opposed to the Oslo Peace Accords as well as any land-for-peace settlement. To further complicate matters more illegal Israeli settlements were constructed in occupied Palestinian areas under Barak than under any other Israeli Prime Minister.

The negotiations also broke down at Camp David between Barak and Arafat largely over the failure of the parties to reach an agreement on the right of refugees to return to Palestinian territories. The Palestinians want to secure the rights of some four million Palestinian refugees worldwide to return to an independent Palestinian state. Professor Elaine C. Hagopian of Simmons College wrote in a *Boston Globe* column,

> Final status negotiations were set in July 2000 at Camp David. Arafat was told to sign away Palestinian rights to fully sovereign statehood and refugee return. Having given in to US-Israeli pressure on interim agreements, his refusal to sign was interpreted as some sort of ploy. The so-called concessions by Barak had two problems: As an occupying power, 'concessions' were not Israel's to make; and close examination of the 'generous concessions' announced in the media show the profile of bantustans choked by Israeli settlements, roads, and border controls.[11]

Professor Hagopian continues,

> The Jerusalem 'concessions' were all fluff, no substance. In return, Barak expected Arafat to be complicit in denying the inalienable rights of Palestinian refugees, 70 percent of the Palestinian population.[12]

Robert Malley, who served as Special Assistant to President Clinton for Arab-Israeli Affairs, was a member of the U.S. peace team and participated in the summit at Camp David, claimed that the Israelis and Palestinians each came to Camp David with very different perspectives which complicated the discussions. Malley confirms that Barak's wavering and lack of leadership skills contributed significantly to the collapse of the Camp David Peace Talks. Malley writes,

> To begin, Barak discarded a number of interim steps, even those to which Israel was formally committed by various agreements - including a third partial redeployment of troops from the West Bank, the transfer to Palestinian control of three villages abutting Jerusalem, and the release of Palestinians imprisoned for acts committed before the Oslo Agreement...Oslo was being turned on its head.[13]

One of Barak's own government Ministers, Haim Ramon, stated in a March 2, 2001 interview, "Ehud was actually against Oslo; his government abandoned the path for peace."[14]

Former U.S. Ambassador Martin Indyk has blamed both Palestinian and Israeli leaders for failing to reach a permanent peace settlement. Indyk has stated further that he does not expect a permanent peace settlement to be reached anytime in the foreseeable future.[15] This represents a severe setback and a sad state of affairs for Israelis and Palestinians. Both sides need to come to terms with each other, put aside their differences and the violence, implement prior agreements, and negotiate a final settlement that guarantees security and autonomy for both sides.

It was further reported that in attempting to secure a peace accord, the Barak government had offered to hand over about ninety-five percent of the West Bank and all of Gaza, a division of Jerusalem, and the removal of some Israeli settlements from Palestinian areas.[16] This information, as reported in many leading news media outlets, is incorrect according to Rachelle Marshall of the International Jewish Peace Union. According to Marshall, the offer Barak made to the Palestinians "was far short of what they could accept. The map [offered by Israel] showed the settlement blocs that Barak insisted upon annexing to Israel extending like thick fingers across the West Bank from Jerusalem to Jericho...What remained to the Palestinians would be three segments of land, each one surrounded by Israeli settlements and roads."[17] Marshall observed, "Barak was hailed in the American press for his willingness to relinquish more territory than any previous prime minister, but his plan would nevertheless have allowed Israel to maintain its grip on the West Bank."[18]

New York University Professor Lev Grinberg has claimed that Barak went to Camp David with the support of only twenty-five percent of the Knesset, knowing that a chance for a settlement was impossible in order to create the myth that a generous offer had been proposed by Israel to the Palestinian Authority.[19]

By the fall and winter of 2000, Barak came under heavy criticism for his poor political skills, lack of effective diplomacy, and inability to end the violence.[20] In addition, Barak worked to expand Jewish settlements in Palestinian areas, continuing the expansion policies of his predecessor, Netanyahu.[21] Violence erupted in late September following a visit by Likud Party Leader Ariel Sharon and his delegation to the Temple Mount, the most sacred religious site to both Jews and Moslems. Reportedly, Sharon, who visited the site armed, had made some controversial remarks regarding the peace process and the status of Jerusalem in the talks. This, along with the failure for a peace agreement to be reached by Barak and Arafat, sparked a new wave of violence against Israel by Palestinian protestors, Intifada II, which had not been seen since the signing of the Oslo Peace Accords in September 1993.

Barak's policies and the failure to reach an agreement at Camp David ignited the Second Intifada, which lasted from September 2000 until 2005. Once again, Palestinian residents engaged in a series of violent and non-violent protests against the Israeli government. This Second Intifada claimed the lives of more than 5,500 Palestinians and 1,100 Israelis and Israeli Arabs.[22] During this time Palestinian militants engaged in a series of suicide bombings against Israelis while Israel responded harshly against these acts of aggression by instituting collective punishment ad home demolitions in the West Bank and Gaza Strip.

Barak was widely viewed as a weak leader because he had also failed to adequately address domestic issues since crime and unemployment soared during his administration.[23] In February 2001, Barak would lose his position as Prime Minister to Likud Party Leader Ariel Sharon, an ardent opponent of the Oslo Accords and the creation of an independent Palestinian state.

NOTES

1. Robert Danin, "A Third Way To Palestine." *Foreign Affairs* (January/February 2011): 97.
2. Ibid.
3. "The Path To Peace Runs Through A History of Turmoil," *CNN.com*. http://www.cnn.com/SPECIALS/2000/mideast/story/overview/ : 1-6.
4. Benjamin Netanyahu, "Palestinians Should Not Have Their Own Nation," in *Israel: Opposing Viewpoints* ed. Charles Cozic, (San Diego: Greenhaven Press, Inc., 1994), 153.
5. Ron Linser, "Role Profile: Benjamin Netanyahu, Israeli Prime Minister." *University of Melbourne*. http://ariel.ucs.unimelb.edu.au/~ronilins/WPT/Profiles/netanyahu.html.
6. American-Israeli Cooperative Enterprise, "The Labor Party Platform," May 1997. http://www.us-israel.org/jsource/politics/labor.html.
7. Benjamin Netanyahu. *A Durable Peace: Israel And Its Place Among The Nations*. (New York: Warner Books, 2000), 162.
8. ABC News, "Ehud Barak." http://www.abcnews.go.com/reference/bios/barak.html.
9. Dr. Mustafa Barghouti, "Why Palestinians Could Not Accept Barak's Proposal," *Arabic Media Internet Network*. http://www.amin.org/En/eyejrs/0105/free3_020501.html: 2.
10. Louis Gerber, "Ariel Sharon: Israel's New Prime Minister," *Cosmopolis*, February 2001. http://www.cosmopolis.ch/english/cosmo14/arielsharon.htm.
11. Elaine C. Hagopian, "The Pope's Emphasis on Palestinian Rights," *The Boston Globe*, May 16, 2001: A15.
12. Ibid.
13. Robert Malley and Hussein Agha, "Camp David: The Tragedy of Errors," *The New York Review*, August 9, 2001: 59.
14. Dr. Ron Pundak, "From Oslo To Taba: What Went Wrong," June 2001. http://www.nahost-politik de/friedensverhandlungen/pundak.htm: 10.
15. Myre, "Departing U.S. Ambassador Faults Israelis, Palestinians," *The Boston Globe*, July 5, 2001: A7.
16. Keith Richburg, "The Palestinians' New Dilemma," *The Washington Post National Weekly Edition*, February 19-25, 2001: 12.
17. Rachelle Marshall, "Is Arafat To Blame For Sharon's Victory? Or Was Defeat 'Barak's and Barak's Alone?,'" *The Washington Report on Middle East Affairs*, April 2001, 6.
18. Ibid; 7.
19. Jane Adas. "Dr. Ghada Karmi, Prof. Lev Grinberg Analyze Post-Oslo Mideast," *Washington Report on Middle East Affairs,* Jan/Feb 2003, 56.
20. Tracy Wilkinson, "The Beginning of the End for Ehud Barak," *Los Angeles Times*, December 1, 2000.
21. "Peace Did Not Fail," *Uri Avnery*, (2001), http://www.gush shalom.org/archives/article131.html.
22. B'Tselem. The Israeli Information Center for Human Rights in The Occupied Territories.http://old.btselem.org/statistics/english/Casualties.asp?sD=29&sM=09&sY=2000&eD=26&eM=12&eY=2008&filterby=event&oferet_stat=before.
23. Louis Gerber, "Ariel Sharon: Israel's New Prime Minister," February 6, 2001. http://www.cosmopolis.ch/english/cosmo14/arielsharon.htm.

Chapter Five

Resurrecting the Oslo Accords

The Mitchell Report

Former President Bill Clinton created a fact-finding commission following the October 2000 Middle East Peace talks held in Sharm-el-Sheikh, Egypt. The role of the Commission was to find out what factors contributed to the renewed violence that followed the failed Peace Talks between Arafat and Barak at Camp David and to explore ways to achieve a permanent settlement between the Israelis and Palestinians. The Commission was chaired by former U.S. Senator George Mitchell (D-ME) and included former U.S. Senator Warren Rudman (R-NH). The Commission's findings were released and made public in May 2001. What has become known as the 'Mitchell Report' concluded, "Fear, hate, anger, and frustration have risen on both sides. The greatest danger of all is that the culture of peace, nurtured over the past decade, is being shattered."[1] The Report continued, "Two proud people share a land and a destiny. Their competing claims and religious differences have led to a grinding, demoralizing, humiliating conflict. They can continue in conflict, or they can negotiate to find a way to live side-by-side in peace."[2] The Mitchell Report explained, "We complied with the request that we would not determine guilt or innocence."[3] The Commission, when established by President Clinton, had been told not to place blame on either party for the escalated violence.

The Mitchell Report stated that "terrorism is reprehensible and unacceptable" and called on the Palestinian Authority to take "immediate steps to apprehend and incarcerate terrorists operating within the PA's [Palestinian Authority's] jurisdiction."[4] The Mitchell Report specifically called for an end to the violence brought on by the Second Intifada and the suicide bombing activities being carried out by Palestinian militants.

The Mitchell Report findings stated that the process that began during the signing of the Oslo Peace Accords has come under intense scrutiny by both the Israeli and Palestinian peoples. It stated, "Both sides see the lack of full compliance with agreements reached since the opening of the peace process as evidence of a lack of good faith. This conclusion led to an erosion of trust even before the permanent-status negotiations began."[5]

The recommendations made by the Mitchell Report were three-fold: 1) End the violence; 2) Rebuild Confidence; and 3) Resume negotiations. In discussing the first recommendation on ending the violence, the Report states that the Israeli government and Palestinian Authority should both act swiftly to stop the violence and reaffirm the commitment to existing agreements in order to begin a series of new negotiations. In considering the second step of rebuilding confidence, the Report recommends a 'cooling-off period' and the implementation of confidence-building measures. This means that both Palestinians and Israelis must acknowledge that acts of violence are unacceptable. In discussing the third step of resuming negotiations, the Report recommends that future negotiations must "manifest a spirit of compromise, reconciliation and partnership, notwithstanding the events of the past seven months."[6] The latter refers to the failure to reach a settlement at Camp David in 2000.

According to the Report, the Palestinian Authority must: 1) Renew cooperation with Israel in order to ensure security guarantees; and 2) Prevent Palestinian gunmen from using Palestinian populated areas to fire upon Israeli populated areas. The Israeli government must: 1) Freeze all settlement activity, including the 'natural growth' of existing settlements; 2) Withdraw military forces to positions held before September 28, 2000, which will reduce the number of violent confrontations; 3) Encourage nonlethal responses to unarmed Palestinian protestors; and 4) Lift closures, transfer all tax revenues owed, and permit Palestinians who work in Israel to return to their jobs.[7]

The Report also acknowledged the political difficulties facing both Israelis and Palestinians. It concluded,

> Israelis do not wish to be perceived as 'rewarding violence.' Palestinians do not wish to be received as 'rewarding occupation.' We appreciate the political constraints of the leaders of both sides. Nevertheless, if the cycle of violence is to be broken and the search for peace resumed, there needs to be a new bilateral relationship incorporating both security cooperation and negotiations.[8]

Then United Nations Secretary-General Kofi Annan expressed optimism about the Mitchell Report findings. Annan stated, "I think there are elements in it which should allow the parties to step back and take steps for a cease-fire, confidence-building measures, and eventually, return to the table."[9]

Shortly after the Report's release, then Palestinian Authority leader Yasir Arafat welcomed the Mitchell Report and called for a summit to be held in order to implement its provisions.[10] In reacting to the Mitchell Report, the Palestinian Authority stated, "The findings and recommendations of the report offer Palestinians and Israelis a sensible and coherent foundation for resolving the current crisis and preparing the path for resuming meaningful negotiations."[11]

The Israeli government responded to the Mitchell Report by demanding that the Palestinians cease all violent actions and uprisings before talks can be convened. On May 21, 2001, in responding to the Mitchell Report, then Israeli Prime Minister Sharon commented, "The Mitchell Report is acceptable to us in principle. We had comments, which we conveyed; and they were clear."[12]

Based upon the information presented here, one can presume that Sharon's conveyed comments probably pertained to his opposition to freezing Israeli settlement expansions in Palestinian territories. Sharon, like Barak and Netanyahu before him, had consistently supported the expansion of Israeli settlements in Palestinian areas. The settlement issue remains a sticking point in negotiations between the Israeli government and Palestinians. Then U.S. Secretary of State Colin Powell commented, "So both sides have commissioned this report, have accepted this report, and it's now time for both sides, with the help of the international community and the United States, to move forward on the basis of this report."[13]

Following publication of the Report, Senator George Mitchell told *Reuters News Agency*, "The United States is a very strong supporter and ally of Israel. But even in such close relationships there are differences of opinion. Every American administration for the past 25 years has opposed the actions and policies of the government of Israel with respect to settlements."[14]

Since Israel has already signed peace agreements with Egypt and Jordan, Syria and Lebanon remain the current bordering nations without an agreement. The dispute between Syria and Israel involves the status of the Golan Heights and access to the Sea of Galilee. The situation in Lebanon is far more complex since that country is still dealing with the consequences of a tragic civil war that lasted from early 1975 to the early 1990's along with numerous other skirmishes since that time. The weakened Lebanese government has been unable to control Palestinian militants, including Hamas and the Islamic Jihad, operating out of southern Lebanon, from attacking Israel or preventing border skirmishes between Israelis and Palestinians. A peace treaty signed by Israel and Jordan allowed for Jordanian control of Muslim holy sites in Jerusalem. Since the government of Jordan has renounced all claims to the West Bank, negotiations and a permanent agreement between the Israeli government and the Palestinian Authority, as well as an agreement with

Syria regarding the Golan Heights, remain most crucial to bringing about stability in the region.

A permanent settlement between the Israelis and Palestinian Authority depends

upon the a resolution of the following important and complex issues between the parties:

1. The status of Israeli settlements in the West Bank and Gaza Strip
2. The return of Palestinian refugees
3. Security guarantees for Israel
4. The creation of an independent Palestinian state with its own police force consistent with United Nations Resolution 181 and 242
5. An agreement on the status of Jerusalem that permits access to all worshippers

As mentioned earlier, United Nations Resolution 181 proposes that the City of Jerusalem be internationalized. This position has also been adopted by the Catholic Church and the Vatican. United Nations Resolution 242 calls upon Israel to withdraw to its 1967 borders and allow for the establishment of an independent Palestinian state in the Gaza Strip and West Bank. The status of Jerusalem will be a major point of contention between both parties. Israeli leaders have declared on a number of occasions that a united Jerusalem will remain under Israeli jurisdiction and control. The issue of Jerusalem is so divisive because of the religious significance and holy sites that this great City contains. Jerusalem has long been a point of contention and battleground for the world's great religions, Judaism, Christianity, and Islam, for over two thousand years. The Israelis want to keep a united Jerusalem as their capital while the Palestinians want to have a portion of Jerusalem as their capital of an independent Palestine.

The present-day Gaza Strip encompasses about three hundred and seventy square miles and approximately 1.7 million people as of 2012. Israel had actually originally promised autonomy to the Gaza Strip region during the 1978 Camp David Accords when it signed a peace treaty with Egypt.[15]

Currently, the number of Palestinian refugees and their descendents in the Israeli-occupied territories totals over four million people.[16] In an interview with *Newsweek* in March 2001, then Prime Minister-Elect Ariel Sharon expressed optimism about his ability to achieve lasting peace with the Palestinians. Sharon stated, "I believe I can make peace because I saw all the horrors of wars. I participated in all the wars and lost my best friends in battles. I was seriously injured twice. Therefore, I understand the importance of peace better than the politicians who speak about peace but never experienced war."[17] Unfortunately, neither peace nor meaningful negotiations occurred during Sharon's tenure as Prime Minister.

Frustration and tensions have been rising on the Palestinian side since the failed Camp David negotiations of 2000 and continuing to the present day. In the spring of 2001, the Fatah, the moderate political movement within the PLO then headed by Arafat and now led by current Palestinian Authority President Mahmoud Abbas, threatened to intensify the Intifada within the territories. In a public statement, Fatah leaders warned, "If Israelis think that Sharon will make security for them, we say loudly that Israel will have no security at all."[18] Both the Palestinians and Israelis have employed terrorist tactics to achieve their goals. Palestinian militants have attacked Israeli civilians and engaged in suicide missions while Israel has employed methods of terrorism in attempting to crush the Palestinian struggle for self-determination and by using methods of torture to extract information. All of these need to stop.

The Israeli government charges that the Palestinian Authority leaders are operating in direct violation of their promises. They point to statements by Palestinian Authorities, including Arafat himself prior to his death in 2004. In 1997, for example, Arafat declared, "The [Israeli] settlements are a declaration of total war against the Palestinian people."[19] A similar comment was made by Farrouk Kaddumi, the head of PLO's Fatah. Kaddumi stated, "The only option in this situation is to continue the Uprising since this is the only language that Israel understands."[20] Peaceful demonstrations by Palestinians to protest deplorable living conditions and to demand autonomy are a recognized form of free expression, however, when these demonstrations result in armed conflict against innocent Israeli civilians, this is a serious and an unacceptable obstacle to peace.

Palestinian observers assert that Palestinian Authority leaders are being forced to bargain from an unfair strength: the use of terrorism. They point to the expansion of Israeli settlements in Palestinian areas, the treatment of Palestinian citizens by Israeli authorities, and the sporadic changes in Israeli government leaders that results in changes in approaches and strategies for reaching a final peace settlement based upon the Oslo Accords. The Israeli government is criticizing Palestinian leaders, including Abbas, for not being forceful enough in controlling Palestinian militants and extremists while at the same time, withholding revenues owed to the Palestinian Authority. The Palestinian Authority is also facing heavy criticism from the radical Hamas, an Islamic Palestinian fundamentalist group that opposes the peace process and the Oslo Accords. Hamas leader Ibrahim Yazaroorie complains that Palestinian leaders and the PLO have "compromised too much" with Israel.[21] Even so, Palestinian Authority leaders must take a more proactive role in condemning hostile propaganda statements directed against Israel by Palestinian radio and newspapers since the spring of 2000. These actions clearly violate the spirit of the Oslo Peace Accords and serve only to disrupt the peace process.

Newsweek correspondent Joshua Hammer has reported that new Israeli checkpoints and blockades have been established in the West Bank with the goal of halting communication between Palestinian leaders. Hammer writes, "The Israeli government insists that a blockade of the West Bank is helping contain the violence, but it may be doing exactly the opposite: intensifying Palestinians' economic misery and rage, while failing for the most part to prevent a determined terrorist from sneaking into the country."[22] In response to violent protests and attacks by Palestinians, the Israeli government has engaged in a policy of increasing Israeli settlements in Palestinian areas and demolishing the homes of Palestinian civilians and families.[23]

Angry Palestinians maintain that American financial assistance to Israel has resulted in American tax dollars paying for bombs and weaponry that Israel uses against Palestinians. Palestinian leaders argue that Israel's dependence on American financial, moral, and political support puts the United States in an ideal position to help facilitate a permanent agreement. The Palestinian Authority also claims that the Clinton administration previously established a role for the United States Government as the mediator and that the United States should assume responsibility and live up to its previous commitments and obligations.[24] Mahmoud Abbas, then a senior Palestinian leader in the West Bank and now President of the Palestinian Authority, has stated, "The American role is not enough and not acceptable. We need American intervention now."[25]

The Israeli government under Sharon was asking that the United States continue to assist Israel financially and politically while maintaining a hands-off approach to the peace process. The current Israeli government and its supporters argue that negotiations between Israel and the Palestinians encompass an internal matter that should be resolved by the parties themselves since the United States is not directly affected by the process itself. Sharon wanted the United States to remove itself from the negotiations and take a backseat role in the Middle East peace process.[26] This approach is favored still by current Israeli Prime Minister Benjamin Netanyahu.

Regarding the ethical question of "Does the United States have a moral obligation to help mediate the Middle East peace process," I would answer Yes. The international community and the United Nations have recognized the existence of the Palestinian Authority and have called for the creation of an independent Palestinian state to coexist alongside the state of Israel. The most important justification for my reasoning is that the United States already assumed responsibility for facilitating this role. In foreign affairs, it is important that we live up to and keep our commitments. Besides, it was the mediation efforts of the United States that led to the signing of the Oslo Peace Accords in the first place.

In addition to the issue of Jerusalem, the Palestinians complain that peace negotiations have dragged on since 1993 without a final agreement and that because of this they reject the new long-term interim agreements proposed by Israel.[27] Palestinian leaders have consistently demanded an end to Israeli settlement expansions in Palestinian territories. The United States government and the world community have publicly acknowledged that the continuing expansion of Israeli settlements in Palestinian territories constitutes a major obstacle to reaching a final peace agreement between the Israeli government and the Palestinian Authority.

CIA Director George Tenet arranged a cease-fire between Israel and the Palestinians on June 12, 2001. The so-called Tenet Plan required Israel to pull back its military troops from Palestinian areas to be relocated to positions they held in September 2000. The Tenet Plan also required the Palestinian Authority to enforce the cease-fire, resume security cooperation with the Israeli government, arrest Palestinian militants from the extremist groups Hamas and Islamic Jihad, and to collect illegal weapons. Although Arafat accepted this proposal at the time, many other Palestinian leaders voiced strong opposition to it and demanded that the full Mitchell Report be incorporated into any cease-fire arrangement.[28]

The Israeli government also complained that Arafat and now Abbas have been unable or unwilling to control Palestinian militants from attacking Israel since the cease-fire was arranged. This is true but by closing Palestinian police posts, holding tax revenues, and refusing to provide adequate resources to the Palestinian Authority, the Israeli government has complicated the tensions and made it all the more difficult for the Palestinian Authority to control the militants. Militant Palestinian groups, who oppose peace with Israel, are gaining support and popularity among Palestinians because of the current state of affairs. Again, Abbas and the Palestinian Authority still has a responsibility to speak out against and strongly condemn Palestinian militants utilizing terrorism against innocent civilians as a retaliatory measure but, Israel too must accept his share of responsibility for escalating tensions.

Palestinian security officers claim that their ability to halt attacks against Israel is limited. Jibril Rajoub, the Palestinian Authority's West Bank Security Chief claims that only eighteen percent of the West Bank is under his jurisdiction and he can only control these areas. Rajoub further maintains that the Palestinian Authority has control only over the areas under his jurisdiction. When questioned as to if the Palestinian Authority has started to re-arrest people who have committed acts of terrorism against Israel, Rajoub responded, "If the Israelis arrest the settlers and soldiers who have killed innocent Palestinians during the last six months, I think it is fair to ask the Palestinians to do the same."[29] This again illustrates the difficulty and complexity of the problem of achieving cooperation on both sides.

The Palestinian Authority has repeatedly requested third party intervention to observe and help resolve the dispute between Israelis and Palestinians. Arafat, and now Abbas, has called for an international peacekeeping force to observe the West Bank and Gaza Strip.[30] This request has been repeatedly rejected by the Israeli government.

In March 2001, the United Nations proposed a resolution backing an observer force for the Palestinians. The resolution called upon United Nations Secretary-General Kofi Annan to work with both parties "on setting up a protection mechanism to contribute to the protection of Palestinian civilians." Exercising its veto power for the first time since 1997, the United States killed the resolution.[31] A voluntary international peacekeeping force would be beneficial since it could objectively monitor the situation in the region while peace negotiations are taking place.

Despite demands from the United States to halt Israeli settlements in Palestinian areas, Israeli leaders have vowed to continue expanding these settlements. As then Prime Minister, Sharon declared, "We will build. Homes will be built in accordance with our current needs."[32] Hundreds of millions of dollars have been expended for the construction of new homes and Jewish settlements in order to accommodate what the Israeli government refers to as 'natural growth' of existing communities.[33] Current Israeli Prime Minister Benjamin Netanyahu is continuing these policies.

The United States has called the Israeli policies and practices of home demolition "provocative." Then State Department Spokesman Richard Boucher, under former President George W. Bush, called on Israel to stop demolishing the homes of Palestinian civilians. Boucher stated, "Actions such as these are provocative and undermine relations between the parties and can only make more difficult efforts to restore calm."[34]

The Vatican has also called upon the Israeli government to withdraw from Palestinian territories, accept U.N. Resolutions, abide by the principles of the Geneva Convention, and recognize the right of the Palestinians to self-determination.[35]

Since his defeat for re-election as Prime Minister, Ehud Barak has been blaming Arafat and the Palestinian Authority leadership for the failure of the parties to reach an agreement. The truth is Barak is trying to cover for his own shortcomings and failures by blaming others. The fact that the Israeli election in February 2001 resulted in the lowest voter-turnout in Israel's history speaks for itself about the quality of the candidates, namely Barak and Sharon.

The Israeli government has also been following a policy of targeting Palestinian police posts for shelling. This obviously further weakens the ability of the Palestinian Authority leaders who want peace, to control the militants and terrorists. Conservative factions in Israel have been calling for a full-scale military invasion of Palestinian territories in the West Bank and Gaza Strip in order to suppress the Palestinian uprising.

The only way to achieve a lasting peace between Israelis and Palestinians is for both parties to acknowledge and guarantee security for Israel as well as the right of Palestinians to self-determination and statehood in the West Bank and Gaza Strip. These were the driving principles rooted in the provisions of the Oslo Peace Accords.

NOTES

1. "The Mitchell Report on the Mideast," *The Miami Herald*, May 17, 2000.
2. Ibid.
3. Ibid.
4. Herb Keinon, "Israel Welcomes Mitchell Report," *The Jerusalem Post*, May 22, 2001. http://www.jpost.com/Editions/2001/05/22/News/News.26707.html.
5. "The Mitchell Report on the Mideast," *The Miami Herald*, May 17, 2000.
6. Ibid.
7. Ibid.
8. Ibid.
9. "Palestinians, Israelis Accept Mitchell Report But Violence Continues," CNN.com/Transcripts, May 21, 2001. http://transcripts.cnn.com/TRANSCRIPTS/0105/21/lt.09.html
10. "Colin Powell's Comments on Mideast," *Associated Press*, 21 May 2001. Available: http://dailynews.yahoo.com/h/ap/20010521/wl/powell_text_3.html.
11. Ibid.
12. Keinon, "Israel Welcomes Mitchell Report."
13. "Colin Powell's Comments on Mideast," *Associated Press*, 21 May 2001.
14. Keinon, "Israel Welcomes Mitchell Report."
15. Learning Network (2000), "The Gaza Strip," *The World & News*. Http://www.factmonster.com/ce6/world/A0858346: 2.
16. United States Census Bureau. http://www.census.gov/population/international/.
17. Larry Weymouth, "I Can Make Peace," *Newsweek*, March 19, 2001, 36-37.
18. Lee Hockstader, "A New Day In Israel," p. 17.
19. Israeli Government Printing Office. 1997. *Palestinian Incitement To Violence Since Oslo: A Four-Year Compendium*, 1.
20. Ibid; 7.
21. Mark Perry, *A Fire In Zion: The Israeli-Palestinian Search For Peace* (New York: William Marrow and Company, 1994), 223.
22. Joshua Hammer, "Israel's Unpluggable Palestinian Problem," *Newsweek*, March 19, 2001: 38.
23. Dan Ephron, "Israeli Tanks Raid Palestinian Camp," *The Boston Globe*, April 12, 2001.
24. Dan Ephron, "U.S. Policy in Israel Viewed As Unfair," *The Boston Globe*, April 5, 2001.
25. Elena Becatoros, "Amid the Violence, Israelis and Palestinians Hold Talks," *The Boston Globe*, April 5, 2001, A13.
26. Jonathan Wright, "Israel Seeks Reduced US Role In Mideast Talks," *The Boston Globe*, May 3, 2001, A18.
27. Greg Myre, "Departing U.S. Ambassador Faults Israelis, Palestinians."
28. Dan Ephron, "U.S. Brokers A Cease-Fire In Mideast," *The Boston Globe*, June 13, 2001, A1, A26.
29. Lally Weymouth, "This Can't Go On," *Newsweek*, July 2, 2001, 29.
30. Greg Myre, "Departing U.S. Ambassador Faults Israelis, Palestinians," *The Boston Globe*, 5 July 2001, A7.
31. Chris Hawley, "U.S. Vetoes U.N. Resolution Backing An Observer Force For Palestinians," *The Lowell Sun*, March 28, 2001, 3.
32. Charles Sennott, "Sharon Defiant on Settlements," *The Boston Globe*, May 9, 2001, A1.
33. Ibid.
34. Dan Ephron, "Israel Destroys Refugee Homes," *The Boston Globe*, July 10, 2001.

35. Elaine C. Hagopian, "The Pope's Emphasis on Palestinian Rights," *The Boston Globe*, May 16, 2001: A15.

Chapter Six

Israel's Policy of Unilateral Disengagement

There have been numerous peace initiatives following the signing of the Oslo Accords in 1993. These include Camp David, Taba, The Road Map, and The Geneva Initiative among others. Unfortunately, all of these initiatives have ended in dismal failure.

On November 28, 2000, the Israeli Knesset voted overwhelmingly to dissolve itself which paved the way for early elections for Prime Minister to be scheduled in February 2001. At that point in time, Barak had served as Prime Minister for just a year and a half. In Israel's February 6, 2001 election, Ariel Sharon defeated Ehud Barak 62.5% to 37.4% in the election for Prime Minister. Sharon won his election over Barak in the lowest voter turnout in Israeli history. Sixty-two percent of eligible Israelis voted compared to the average turnout of eighty percent. Sharon had been considered one of Israel's most controversial military and political leaders. He too had an extensive military and political career prior to assuming his new position. Sharon had previously served as Chairman of Israel's Likud Party. He was viewed as a hardliner in Israeli politics and was an outspoken critic of the Oslo Peace Accords. In campaigning for Prime Minister, Sharon had promised "peace with security."[1]

Sharon had announced his intentions to run against Prime Minister Ehud Barak in the February 2001 elections on November 28, 2000, the same day that the Israeli Knesset voted to dissolve itself. In making his announcement, Sharon stated his purpose for running was to halt what he viewed as further concessions to the Palestinians in peace negotiations. Sharon argued against a final peace agreement encompassing an exchange of land for peace. Instead, Sharon proposed an interim pact on what he called non-belligerence. At that time, a Likud Party challenge was expected from former Prime Minister Benjamin Netanyahu, however, a procedural clause in Israel's parliamentary government ended up preventing Netanyahu's candidacy. Sharon claimed that he liked Barak personally but that, Barak lacked political experience and was thus incapable of finalizing a long-term peace agreement with the Palestinians. It is perhaps worth mentioning that Ehud Barak was given the rank of brigadier-general of the Israeli army by Sharon decades earlier.[2] Sharon had stated, "I am for a lasting peace...I believe that I understand the importance of peace better than many of the politicians who speak about peace but never had that experience. For me, peace should provide security to the Jewish people and peace for generations."[3]

When Ariel Sharon joined Israel's ruling Likud Party government in 1977, he worked to secure Israel's dominance over the West Bank and its water supply.[4] Throughout the 1970's, 1980's, and 1990's, Sharon had encouraged the construction of Israeli settlements in strategic areas of the West Bank which could be connected by highways to Israel that bypassed Palestinian cities and towns.[5] Sharon's goal was to isolate the Palestinian population around Israeli settlements and outposts.[6]

Sharon was a fierce opponent of engaging in negotiations with the PLO. In his best-selling book, *From Beirut to Jerusalem*, Thomas Friedman claims that by invading Beirut in 1982, Sharon was hoping to force the then 1.7 million Palestinians living in the West Bank and Gaza Strip to abandon their pursuit of an independent Palestinian state by destroying their representative, the Palestine Liberation Organization [PLO], and accepting limited autonomy granted by Israel. This would allow Israel to forever retain control over the West Bank and Gaza.[7]

In place of the Oslo Accords, Sharon proposed that a four-fold plan be initiated in areas handed over to the Palestinians: 1) Israel will demand the correction of all violations which must encompass an all-out war by the Palestinian Authority against terrorism; 2) The extradition of wanted murderers; 3) Confiscation of all firearms and weapons; and 4) An end to anti-Israel incitement. In territories that have not yet been handed over to the Palestinians, Sharon states, that the Likud Plan will be implemented. No more land will be turned over to the Palestinian Authorities. Sharon further argued that the Jewish settlements and other security areas must remain under exclusive Israeli control. He wrote, "In addition, the main arteries connecting the coastal plain with the Jordan River and the Dead Sea will be included in the security areas, and several kilometers on each side of them."[8] To achieve a real and lasting peace with the Palestinians, Israel's leaders need to be more flexible with regards to territorial concessions.

As Prime Minister from 2001-2005, Ariel Sharon adopted what he called "Unilateral Disengagement." As part of his policy to disengage with the Palestinians, Sharon dismantled Israeli settlements in the Gaza Strip. As a result, approximately 8,000 Israeli settlers were relocated.[9] Although the dismantlement of the settlements was a welcome development, they were paved with bad intentions. Not only did Sharon and the Israeli government make these moves unilaterally, they removed the settlements in order to prevent the peace process and a permanent settlement from resuming. This was confirmed by Rabbi Bruce Warshal, publisher of the Broward Jewish Journal of South Florida. Rabbi Warshal quotes Dov Wesiglass, Sharon's senior advisor, as stating, "The disengagement (from Gaza) is actually formaldehyde. It supplies the amount of formaldehyde that is necessary so that there will not be a political process with the Palestinians… this whole package that is called the Palestinian state has been removed from our agenda indefinitely."[10] It is worth noting that current Israeli Prime Minister Benjamin Netanyahu resigned his position as Finance Minister in Sharon's government in protest of Israel's dismantlement of the Gaza settlements.

Construction of new Israeli settlements in the West Bank and East Jerusalem continued following the collapse of peace talks at Camp David in 2000. Since acquiring East Jerusalem and the West Bank in 1967, Israel has built homes for 470,000 Israelis there. From 2006 to 2009, during the Olmert Administration, 5,100 Israeli homes were built in the West Bank and another 560 buildings were constructed illegally in unauthorized outposts in the West Bank. Palestinian leaders have consistently demanded an end to the settlement construction in order for negotiations to resume.

Under Sharon, Israel constructed a 420-mile separation barrier through the West Bank and parts of Jerusalem. The stated purpose of the barrier wall was to keep out suicide bombers from Israel.[11] This West Bank barrier has consumed more than 8.5% of West Bank Palestinian land. According to *Time* magazine, "The economic consequences of the Wall are plain: it has kept out of Israel hundreds of thousands of Palestinians who used to travel there every day, mostly to work."[12]

In addition, the border between the Gaza Strip and Egypt has been sealed off preventing trade or travel.[13] In 2010, after facing tremendous international pressure, Israel announced that it would allow for some supplies to enter Gaza with close monitoring. These include food, medicine, and construction materials to build houses and schools which are desperately needed in Gaza.

In 2004, Palestinian Authority Leader Yasir Arafat, who had been confined to his compound by Israeli military forces under orders from Sharon and the Israeli Government, which accused Arafat of inciting violence against Israel, became ill and died at age 75 following a brief coma on November 11, 2004. His exact cause of death is unknown since an autopsy was never performed. Many suspect that Arafat was poisoned. He was replaced by his former Prime Minister Mahmoud Abbas, who was elected democratically by the Palestinians the following year. Abbas has served as President of the Palestinian Authority since this time and elections scheduled for 2009 have been constantly postponed by the Palestinian Authority.

Ariel Sharon was left in a coma following a stroke that he suffered in early 2005. His Deputy Prime Minister, Ehud Olmert, succeeded him as Prime Minister. Olmert served as Prime Minister until 2009, when he was replaced in Israel's elections by Likud Party activist Benjamin Netanyahu, another vocal opponent of the Oslo Peace Accords and a Palestinian state situated in the Gaza Strip and West Bank. As discussed earlier, Netanyahu previously served as Prime Minister from 1996 to 1999 and during this time had worked tirelessly to dismantle the Oslo Peace Accords. Prior to this Olmert, whose administration had been under investigation for bribery and political corruption, stated that he supported a two-state solution leading to Palestinian independence. Olmert, it should be pointed out, was the only Likud member of Parliament to vote to give the Palestinians self-rule autonomy in the West Bank in 1987.[14] It is also known that Olmert had planned to incorporate between 10-15% of Palestinian land in the West Bank into the separation barrier of Greater Israel.[15]

NOTES

1. "The Path To Peace Runs Through A History of Turmoil," *CNN.com*. http://www.cnn.com/SPECIALS/2000/mideast/story/overview/ : 1.
2. William Maclean, "Sharon To Stand Against Barak In Israel Polls," Reuters, November 29, 2000. http://uk.news.yahoo.com/001129/80/aqfu7.html.
3. Ariel Sharon, "I Am For A Lasting Peace," November 14, 2000. http://www.freeman.org/m_online/dec00/sharon.htm.
4. Rachelle Marshall, "U.S. and Israel Confront Middle East Realities," The Washington Report on Middle East Affairs, September/October 2007, 7.
5. Ibid.
6. Ibid.
7. Thomas L. Friedman. *From Beirut To Jerusalem* (New York: Farrar Straus Giroux, 1989), 268-269.
8. Ariel Sharon, "The Likud's Plan, Simply Put," The Jerusalem Post, June 1996. http://www.freeman.org/m_online/jun96/sharon1.htm.
9. Rachelle Marshall, "U.S. and Israel Confront Middle East Realities," 7.
10. Rabbi Bruce Warshal, "Who Started This War?" Broward Jewish Journal, January 15, 2009, 22.
11. Dan Ephron, "Breaching The Barrier," Newsweek, December 19, 2005, 48.
12. Karl Vick and Ein Arik, "Palestinians Contained." Time, December 20, 2010, 51.
13. Mohammed Daraghmeh, "After Losses, Palestinian Zeal For Intifadah Flongs," Boston Sunday Globe, September 30, 2007, A17.
14. Kevin Peraino, "The Making of A Candidate," Newsweek, January 23, 2006, 32.
15. Rachelle Marshall, "Olmert's Separation Plan Would End Hope For A Palestinian State," The Washington Report on Middle East Affairs. April 2006, 8.

Chapter Seven

Palestinian Elections and New Tensions with Israel

The Oslo Peace Accords established the office of a democratically elected President of a new Palestinian Authority with a democratic Parliament consisting of 132 seats. The five major Palestinian political parties are: 1) Fatah; 2) Reform and Change [Hamas]; 3) Third Way; 4) Popular Front for the Liberation of Palestine; and 5) Independent Palestine. Fatah is the party formerly led by Arafat and currently led by Mahmoud Abbas. Third Way was organized by former Palestinian Finance Minister Salam Fayyad. Independent Palestine is led by Mustafa Barghouti, a human rights activist and cousin to popular Fatah militant Marwan Barghouti, who is serving a life prison sentence in Israel for instigating Palestinian attacks on that nation.[1]

There is no question that the Palestinian Authority previously under the leadership of Yasir Arafat has been plagued by corruption and scandal. Under Arafat's leadership, the Palestinian economy had declined greatly, the Gross Domestic Product [GDP] had fallen by 70 percent, the public infrastructure has collapsed, and public health standards have fallen dramatically. This is despite the fact that the Palestinian Authority has received billions of dollars in financial assistance from the international community, including the United States. In 1997, the Palestinian Authority received more than $100 billion dollars in international assistance and Palestinian tax revenues. By the end of the year, $323 million dollars was unaccounted for in the Palestinian Authority's annual report. Another example of Palestinian Authority mismanagement is of $20 million dollars that had been given to the Palestinian Mortgage Housing Corporation by the European Union for the purpose of building low-cost housing in the Gaza Strip for the Palestinian population. The European Union later discovered that the funds had been used to build luxury housing for supporters of Yasir Arafat. It was also documented that Arafat deposited over $5 million dollars in Arab nation assistance to the Palestinian Authority into his personal account.[2]

These activities and mismanagement on the part of the Palestinian Authority have also stifled the peace process by creating a loss of confidence on the part of many Israelis, Palestinians, and members of the international community in the ability of the Palestinian Authority to properly manage resources on behalf of the Palestinian people. It could also be argued that these failures by the Palestinian Authority have contributed to the creation and popularity of Palestinian resistance movements opposing the peace process and engaging in terrorist attacks against the Israeli people.

In January 2006, Hamas won a major victory in the Palestinian Parliament. The election followed enormous pressure applied by then President George W. Bush for the Palestinian Authority to hold free and fair elections. Hamas candidates running on the Reform and Change ticket won 74 of the 132 seats in Parliament while Fatah won just 45. The other minor parties and Independents control the remaining 13 seats. After its win, Hamas Leader Mahmoud Zahar remarked, "The people will be rid of the disgusting situation that they live in-the corruption within the weak and ineffective PA [Palestinian Authority] that can' even bring itself to arrest drug addicts, let alone other criminals."[3]

After Hamas won a majority in the Palestinian Parliament, it resulted in its political leader, Ismail Haniyeh, becoming Prime Minister under Palestinian Authority President Mahmoud Abbas. Hamas thus replaced the more moderate Fatah as the dominant political party in the Palestinian parliament. As mentioned earlier, Fatah was the political organization of both Arafat and Abbas, which favored direct political negotiations and a peaceful settlement with Israel leading to a two-state solution for Israelis and Palestinians. The United States and the European Union immediately boycotted the new Palestinian government both politically and financially following the victory of Hamas leaders.

The recognized leader of Hamas is Khaled Mashaal who resides in Damascus, Syria and serves as Chairman of the Hamas Political Bureau. The political leader of Hamas is Dr. Mahmoud Zahar, who founded the political organization of the wing that was elected to the Palestinian Parliament. Sheikh Hassan Yousef remains the most significant leader of Hamas in the West Bank and holds a seat in the Palestinian Parliament. Ismail Haniyeh is the most visible political figure in Hamas. Haniyeh leads the Hamas delegation in Parliament and is viewed as a moderate who favors negotiations with Israel.[4]

There were a total of 1,011,992 Palestinians voters who voted in the Palestinian elections, which is approximately 74.6% of all registered Palestinian voters.[5] Palestinians were angered by deteriorating economic conditions in the territories under the leadership of Fatah. For example, there was a

35% decline in gross domestic product between 2000 and 2005 in the Gaza Strip and West Bank. The stated goal of Hamas is to eradicate Israel and establish an Islamic military state throughout the West Bank, Gaza Strip, and Israel. The Hamas victory ended 40 years of Fatah dominance over the leadership of the Palestinian people.[6]

M.J. Rosenberg, the Director of the Israeli Forum's Office in Washington D.C. observed regarding the Hamas victories, "The fact is that it was eminently predictable and perhaps even inevitable in the sense that the actions of Fatah, the Americans, and the Israelis made it so."[7]

Rosenberg further argues, "The Palestinians were tired of Fatah's corruption and cronyism."[8] Rosenberg maintains that the Bush Administration in allowing then Prime Minister Ariel Sharon to do what he wished and to act unilaterally created the climate and conditions for a Hamas victory in the Palestinian Parliamentary elections in January 2006.[9]

Both the Bush Administration and now the Obama Administration have maintained that it cannot deal with Hamas as a political organization because its charter calls for the destruction of Israel as a nation-state. On June 16, 2007, Former U.S. President Jimmy Carter observed, "The United States and Israel decided to punish all the people in Palestine and did everything they could to deter compromise between Hamas and Fatah."[10] President Carter has advocated that the United States, Israel, and the international community promote cooperation and collaboration between Fatah and Hamas leading up to a peace settlement between the Palestinians and Israel.

Shortly after taking office as Prime Minister of the Palestinian Authority following an invitation by Palestinian Authority President Mahmoud Abbas after the Hamas Parliamentary victory in January 2006, Ismail Haniyeh cut his own salary from $4,000 per month to $1,500 per month in U.S. dollars to set the tone for a reform agenda.[11]

In June 2006, Haniyeh brokered an agreement with Abbas promising to recognize the State of Israel, which the Hamas Charter has pledged to destroy, provided that Israel withdraw to its pre-1967 borders. Haniyeh's move angered Hamas hardliners who want to eradicate Israel completely.[12] Most would agree that this was certainly a positive step in the right direction.

On several occasions, Haniyeh has indicated that Hamas may be receptive towards recognizing Israel and renouncing violence once Israel acknowledges the rights of the Palestinian people and agrees to the creation of an independent Palestinian state. Haniyeh has stated, "We are not war seekers nor are we war initiators. We are not lovers of blood. We are oppressed people with rights. If peace brings us our rights, then this is good."[13] Haniyeh has commented further, "If Israel returns to the '67 borders, then we will establish peace in stages and that a two-state solution "starts with Israel."[14]

Despite Haniyeh's statements, the fact remains that the Hamas Charter favors a unified Islamic state in Israel and Palestine with Jews and Christians living under Islamic rule.[15] This position obviously needs to be abandoned through negotiations if a meaningful peace settlement is to come to fruition. Palestinian Authority President Mahmoud Abbas has demanded consistently that Hamas renounce the use of violence, recognize Israel as a nation-state, and acknowledge all existing agreements between Israel and the Palestine Liberation Organization [PLO].[16] This too will need to happen before a final-status settlement is reached between Israel and the Palestinians. At the same time, Article 9 of the PLO Charter states that armed struggle is the only way to liberate occupied Palestine from Israel. This provision will also need to be eliminated for a peace settlement to be possible.

Following the victory of Hamas in Palestinian parliamentary elections in January 2006, international contributors cut off over $1.6 billion in aid to the Palestinian Authority. Over 165,000 teachers, nurses, and other government officials went unpaid. The wages of public employees sustain nearly a third of the Palestinian population.[17]

Israel is responsible for collecting customs fees in the Palestinian territories, which amounts to about $700 million per year. These customs constitute the primary revenue for the Palestinian Authority Government.[18] Since the Hamas victory, Israel has withheld much of these revenues. More than half of the Palestinian Authority's $3 billion annual budget comes from foreign countries, including the United States.[19]

Although Hamas leaders have stated that they will not recognize Israel's right to exist as a Jewish state until Israel agrees to return the West Bank and Gaza Strip, Fatah leader Sami Masharawi observed, "Hamas has recognized a state in the '67 borders."[20]

Hamas had maintained a ceasefire with Israel from March 2005 until June 2006. On June 25, 2006, Hamas militants killed two Israeli soldiers after digging through a fence on the Gaza Strip and kidnapped Israeli Corporal Gilad Shalit.[21] After nearly five years of captivity, Shalit was released in October 2011 as part of a prisoner exchange agreed to between Israel and Hamas. 1,027 Palestinian prisoners were released by Israel in return for Shalit, the highest number of prisoners ever exchanged for a single Israeli soldier. Although the agreement was facilitated by German and Egyptian mediators it proves that negotiations between Israel and Hamas can lead to a desirable outcome for both sides.

Hezbollah, or Party of God, was created in 1982 as a Shiite resistance group to oppose Israel's invasion of Southern Lebanon, which had occurred earlier that year.[22] Hezbollah claimed a historic victory when Israeli military forces withdrew from Southern Lebanon in 2000.[23] Sheikh Hasan Nasrallah, the leader of Hezbollah, declared a "divine victory" against Israel.[24]

After Israel withdrew its forces from most of Southern Lebanon, Hezbollah had been allowed to retain its arms and weapons since that time. The issue of whether or not Hezbollah should remain an armed militia group has been a very politically divisive issue inside Lebanon. Israel has demanded that the Lebanese government take proactive steps to completely disarm Hezbollah. Lebanon's national army has been unable to manage Hezbollah militants because it has been left in a weakened state following Lebanon's 15-year civil war and the withdrawal of Syrian forces from that country in 2005. Both Syria and Iran have provided economic and military assistance to Hezbollah since its creation and both countries continue to aid the organization presently.[25]

The actions of Hamas in June 2006 had served to provoke Hezbollah in July 2006 to carry out an offensive against Israel. The stated goal of the offensive operations by both groups was to secure a prisoner exchange with Israel.[26] Israel had participated in prisoner exchanges with both Hezbollah and Hamas in the past. In 2004, Israel released 424 prisoners in return for the remains of three Israeli soldiers and a captured Israeli businessman. Between 2004 and 2006, Israel had arrested and detained more than 9,000 Palestinian and Lebanese militants. If either Hamas or Hezbollah succeeded in securing the release of militants held by Israel, they would gain hero status in the Palestinian territories.[27] Hezbollah leader Hasan Nasrallah seeks grandeur status in both the Arab world and in Lebanon's Palestinian refugee camps.

Israel and Hezbollah ended up in a full-scale war during the Summer of 2006 after Hezbollah forces in Lebanon invaded Northern Israel. This invasion followed Hezbollah bombing raids on Israel from the Lebanese border. Israel's Summer 2006 bombardment of Lebanon occurred following Hezbollah's kidnapping of two Israeli soldiers on the border. The abduction of these two soldiers came just two weeks after Hamas militants abducted Israeli corporal Gilad Shalit and took him into the Gaza Strip.[28]

Hezbollah had also killed several dozen Israelis and terrorized hundreds of thousands more by initiating rocket missile attacks into Israel. It initiated the fighting with Israel after raiding the country on July 12, 2006 and killing 8 Israeli soldiers.[29]

The war between Israel and Hezbollah lasted for 34 days. The fighting resulted in the deaths of 41 Israeli civilians and 117 Israeli troops. During this time, Hezbollah militants fired over 4,000 rockets into Israel. The Israeli response on Hezbollah resulted in more than 900 civilian deaths in southern Lebanon and left thousands of people homeless. The Israeli campaign also destroyed billions of dollars in Lebanese infrastructure.[30]

Paul Salem, the Director of the Carnegie Middle East Center in Beirut, maintains that the Iranian-supported Hezbollah raid into Israel was intended to draw that nation into a short battle on the northern Lebanese border and to facilitate a prisoner exchange between the two countries at the same time the White House was criticizing Iran for its uranium enrichment program and nuclear ambitions.[31]

Israel's offensive ultimately failed to root out Hezbollah and eradicate the group's militants. Arguably, the offensive has actually bolstered Hezbollah's popularity with Palestinian refugees in southern Lebanon and throughout the Palestinian territories.[32]

The skirmish was seen largely as a victory for Hezbollah since Israeli airpower failed to halt Hezbollah missile attacks or damage Hezbollah strongholds.[33] Gen. Dan Halutz, Chief of Israeli defense Forces [IDF], had promised to "turn the clock back 20 years in Lebanon" by destroying that country's infrastructure following the abduction of the two Israeli soldiers by Hezbollah.[34] Gen. Halutz was forced to step down as commander of the IDF following the cessation of Israeli military incursions in Lebanon. Gen. Halutz's operations are widely viewed as a failure both inside and outside of Israel.[35] It is also important to note that Israeli airstrikes against Hezbollah have provoked Shiite militants to oppose U.S. interests in the Middle East, especially in Iraq and Afghanistan.

Following Israel's response in South Lebanon in August 2006, more than 700 Lebanese people had been killed. At the same time, more than 150 Palestinians were killed in the Gaza Strip. Most of the people killed were civilians. In addition, hundreds of thousands of Lebanese were made refugees by Israel's actions.[36]

Writer Rachelle Marshall of the Jewish International Peace Union maintains that Israel's invasion of Lebanon and Gaza during the Summer of 2006 was intended to accomplish three major Israeli policy objectives: (1) To prevent the creation of an autonomous Palestinian state; (2) To retain control over the Golan Heights; and (3) To create a favorable government in Lebanon. According to Marshall, "To accomplish these goals the Israelis know they must first eliminate resistance forces such as Hamas and Hezbollah.[37]

In June 2007, Palestinian Authority President Mahmoud Abbas and Hamas leader Ismail Haniyeh pledged to combine their security forces and collaborate on security matters. Later that Summer, Fatah security personnel established independent security posts throughout the Gaza Strip, violating the earlier pact between Fatah and Hamas. This resulted in much street fighting between Fatah and Hamas. Hamas forces seized control over the main security posts in Gaza following a week of severe fighting in June 2007 between Hamas and Fatah. Hamas had forced Fatah security forces to surrender within days and exercised control over all of Gaza by the end of June 2007.[38] It is worth mentioning that approximately 45,000 security forces are employed by Abbas's Palestinian Authority Government. Only about 5,000 of these men resisted Hamas's advances in Gaza.[39]

Hamas leader Ismail Haniyeh granted amnesty to all Fatah operatives and offered to re-establish a unity government with Abbas and Fatah. Abbas refused this arrangement and dismissed Haniyeh as Prime Minister while appointing Fatah-loyalist Salam Fayyad to fill the role. Fayyad is highly respected by many U.S. Government officials in Washington because he was educated in the United States and holds a Ph.D. in Economics.[40]

The fighting that occurred in the Summer of 2007 has left the governing authority of the Palestinians fractured. Hamas is exercising exclusive control over the Gaza Strip with Haniyeh in control while Fatah is governing the West Bank with the Palestinian Authority government headed by President Abbas.[41]

The U.S. and Israel had been pressuring Abbas to dissolve the unity government with Hamas almost immediately following the government's inception. On June 14, 2007, Abbas formally dissolved the national unity government. He also voided all travel documents given in Gaza. In addition, Abbas prohibited and censored all Hamas media outlets in the West Bank.[42]

After the Hamas takeover in Gaza, the organization claimed that it had no political agenda. Hamas officials claimed that they were defending Gaza from segments of Fatah that had refused to share authority and instead had been catering to Israeli and American interests.[43]

Following Hamas's seizure of the Gaza Strip, Haniyeh called for new negotiations with Abbas and Fatah leaders to achieve a "no winner, no loser, a government of national unity."[44] Amnesty was immediately granted afterwards to captured Fatah security fighters. Abbas responded to the Hamas overtures by stating that he would not engage in dialogue with "murderous terrorists."[45] On May 24, 2007, Israel rounded up and arrested 33 prominent Palestinians in the West Bank affiliated with Hamas.[46]

In Gaza, Haniyeh has established a government with himself as the chief authority figure. Mahmoud al-Zahar, a co-founder of Hamas in Gaza, is serving as Haniyeh's Foreign Minister. Mohammed Delf is serving as military commander in charge of security operations in Gaza. Haniyeh answers to Hamas political leader Khaled Mashaal, who resides in exile in Damascus, Syria.[47]

In the West Bank, Abbas has established a new cabinet following the split with Hamas. In June 2007, Abbas appointed Salam Fayyad, a former official of the World Bank who received his Ph.D. in Economics in the United States, as Prime Minister and Abd al-Razzaq al-Yahya, a veteran Palestine Liberation organization leader, as Interior Minister.[48] Fayyad is viewed as a moderate and is well-liked by many in the United States and Europe. Fayyad has a history of combating political corruption within the Palestinian Authority and has been openly critical of Hamas.

Fatah militants in the West Bank have rounded up and arrested hundreds of Hamas members and supporters and have destroyed countless buildings and businesses with Hamas ties. The U.S., Israel, and the European Union have recognized the Palestinian Authority government of Mahmoud Abbas. All refuse to acknowledge Haniyeh or Hamas control over the Gaza Strip.[49]

Following the split between Hamas and the Palestinian Authority, Hamas political leader Khaled Mashaal stated that "Abbas has legitimacy…he is an elected President, and we will cooperate with him in the national interest."[50] Marshaal has also stated that Hamas will honor past agreements it has made with Fatah as well as earlier Palestinian agreements with Israel.[51] At that time Abbas ignored these overtures and refused to reconcile with Hamas leaders.

Although the relationship between the United States and Israel has grew stronger after the September 11th attacks, that relationship has been strained with the election of President Barack Obama in the United States and the election of right-wing Prime Minister Benjamin Netanyahu in Israel in 2008 and 2009.

U.S. policy has been to refuse to hold talks with, much less negotiate with, Hamas. Robert Malley, who served as Special Assistant for Arab-Israeli Security Affairs under President Clinton, maintains that the United States needs to take a leadership role in fostering dialogue between all concerned parties in the Middle East in order to resolve the Israeli-Palestinian dispute.[52]

As political commentator Pat Buchanan observed following the Hamas election victory, "Bush then called for free elections in Palestine, open to all parties. So it came to pass that in February 2006, Hamas triumphed over Fatah."[53] Buchanan further noted, "Instantly, Israel cut off all tax revenue to the Palestinian Authority and demanded Bush halt aid. Meekly, Bush complied, destroying any remnants of his credibility."[54] Buchanan added, "It was said that these Americans support free elections-as long as their side wins. The Palestinians were punished by the United States for having voted wrong."[55]

Council on Foreign Relations President Richard Haas calls for U.S. policymakers to revive diplomatic efforts between Israelis and Palestinians. Haas calls for the creation of an independent "Palestinian state based on the 1967 lines."[56] He claims that the borders will have to be slightly adjusted to ensure Israel's security and to incorporate demographic changes, but that Palestinians would have to be compensated for those adjustments.[57]

According to Haas, "The more generous and detailed the plan, the harder it would be for Hamas to reject negotiation and favor confrontation."[58] Haas recommends that "U.S. officials ought to sit down with Hamas officials in order to win broader support for a peace settlement."[59]

Israel has its fair share of extremist elements as well. The Yisrael Beytenu Party, led by hard-line politician Avigdor Lieberman, holds approximately 15 seats in Israel's Knesset Parliament. Lieberman has advocated expelling Israel's Arab citizens from the country. It should be noted that Israel's Arab citizen population consists of about 1.3 million people and this constitutes approximately 20 percent of Israel's population. Lieberman has been described by Martin Peretz, an avid Zionist critical of the peace process, of *The New Republic* as a "neo-fascist."[60] Liberman is currently serving as Foreign Minister in Netanyahu's government. *Newsweek's* Fareed Zakaria observed, "No liberal democracy I know of since World War II has disenfranchised or expelled its own citizens."[61]

NOTES

1. "Palestinian Elections At A Glance," *Associated Press*, January 23, 2006.
2. "Israel 1991 to Present PA Corruption." Palestinefacts.org.
3. "Extreme Victory," *Newsweek*. February 6, 2006.
4. "Upheaval In The Middle East," *Boston Globe*, January 27, 2006.
5. Matthew Gutman, "Hamas Voters Fed Up With Fatah," *USA Today*, January 27, 2006, 5A.
6. Ibid.
7. M.J. Rosenberg, "Who Elected Hamas," *The American Conservative*, February 27, 2006, 9.
8. Ibid.
9. Ibid.
10. Shawn Pogatchnik, "Carter Blasts U.S. Policy on Palestinians," *Associated Press*, 16 June 16, 2007.
11. Mohammed Omer, "Hamas Forms A Government," *The Washington Report on Middle East Affairs*, May/June 2006, 12.
12. Michael Elliott, "Why They Fight and Why It's Different This Time," *Time,* July 24, 2006, 26.
13. Lally Weymouth, "Not Lovers of Blood," *Newsweek,* March 6, 2006, 30.
14. Ibid.
15. Donald Neff, "Israel Created Two of Its Own Worst enemies – Hamas and Hezbollah," *Washington Report on Middle East Affairs,* November 2002, 21.
16. Lally Weymouth, "Not Lovers of Blood," 30.
17. Rachelle Marshall, "Occupation: The Missing Word," *The Washington Report on Middle East Affairs*, August 2006, 8.
18. "Extreme Victory," *Newsweek,* February 6, 2006, 29.
19. Kevin Peraino, "Palestine's New Perspective," *Newsweek*, September 14, 2009, 44.
20. Rachelle Marshall, "Occupation: The Missing Word," 8.
21. Michael Elliott, "Why They Fight and Why It's Different This Time," *Time*, July 24, 2006, 23.
22. Ibid.
23. Richard Haas, "The New Middle East," *Foreign Affairs*, November/December 2006, 15.
24. Ibid; 18.
25. Michael Elliott, "Why They Fight and Why It's Different This Time," *Time*, 27.
26. Ibid; 26.
27. Ibid; 27.
28. Ibid; 23.
29. Ibid.
30. Richard Walker, "Israeli Report Details Army's Crushing Defeat In Lebanon," *American Free Press*, May 14, 2007, 10.
31. Paul Salem, "The Future of Lebanon," *Foreign Affairs*, November/December 2006, 13.
32. Richard Walker, "Israeli Report Details Army's Crushing Defeat In Lebanon," 10.
33. Richard Haas, "The New Middle East," *Foreign Affairs*, November/December 2006, 3.
34. Richard Walker, "Israeli Report Details Army's Crushing Defeat In Lebanon," 10.
35. Ibid.

36. Matthew Rothschild, "The Israeli-American Invasion," *The Progressive*, September 2006, 8.
37. Rachelle Marshall, "The Real Reason For Israel's Wars on Gaza and Lebanon," *The Washington Report on Middle East Affairs*, September/October 2006, 8.
38. Rachelle Marshall, "U.S. and Israel Confront Middle East Realities," *The Washington Report on Middle East Affairs,* September/October 2007, 7.
39. Tim McGirk, "How To Deal With Hamas," *Time*, July 2, 2007, 27.
40. Ibid; 40.
41. Rachelle Marshall, "U.S. and Israel Confront Middle East Realities," 7.
42. Rachelle Marshall, "The Dangerous Legacy of Occupation." *The Washington Report on Middle East Affairs,* August 2007, 8.
43. Ibid.
44. Ibid.
45. Ibid.
46. Ibid.
47. Tim McGirk, "How To Deal With Hamas," 30.
48. Ibid.
49. Rachelle Marshall, "U.S. and Israel Confront Middle East Realities," 8.
50. Tim McGirk, "How To Deal With Hamas," 32.
51. Ibid; 27.
52. Robert Malley, "Time To Start Talking," *Time*, July 24, 2006, 30.
53. Patrick J. Buchanan, "Are Gazans Now Our Enemies Too?" *The American Conservative*, July 16, 2007, 15.
54. Ibid.
55. Ibid.
56. Richard Haas, "The New Middle East," *Foreign Affairs*, November/December 2006, 11.
57. Ibid.
58. Ibid.
59. Ibid.
60. Fareed Zakaria, "Israel's Biggest Danger." *Newsweek,* February 23, 2009, 41.
61. Ibid.

Chapter Eight

The Road Map to Peace and Alternatives to Oslo

When looking at the current state of affairs, there are five possible outcomes to the Israeli-Palestinian conflict: 1) Status quo with Israel retaining control of the occupied territories; 2) Unification of Israelis and Palestinians into a single nation; 3) Partition into two states, one Jewish, and one Palestinian; 4) Expulsion of Palestinians; and 5) Elimination of Israel. Most observers would probably agree that the first outcome of status quo is likely to prevail since Israel remains very capable of defeating both the Palestinians and the surrounding Arab countries.

Peace did occur with the signing of the Oslo Peace Accords from the fall of 1993 to September 2000. Although there were isolated incidents of aggression on both sides, Israelis and Palestinians for the most part, did live in peace and security without an organized Intifada Uprising. This peace was largely the result of Palestinians witnessing an end to what they viewed as the oppression of Israeli occupiers and the beginning of Palestinian self-rule in the West Bank and Gaza Strip. The failure of both sides to reach a permanent peace agreement rooted in the Oslo Accords helped to ignite another round of Palestinian Uprisings, Intifada II, in September 2000.

The collapse of the Oslo Peace Accords and the subsequent developments in Israel and the Palestinian territories have created a wave of pessimism regarding the possibility of a lasting peace settlement between Israelis and Palestinians. But the voices of peace on both sides remain determined and strong. Several proposals for peace have emerged from Israelis and Palestinians desiring a viable peace settlement.

The fundamental demands of the Palestinians remain the same. These are: (1) An independent Palestinian state located in the West Bank and Gaza Strip with East Jerusalem as the capital; (2) Autonomy over Palestinian borders and economy; and 93) The right of Palestinian refugees displaced after 1947 to return.[1] In addition, consensus must be reached on security guarantees and water rights. Finally, a final status agreement must lead to peace and the normalization of relations between Israel and the other Arab countries in the Middle East with the Arab League playing a crucial role.

During the fall of 2002, then President George W. Bush instructed his foreign policy advisors to draft a blueprint plan for peace in the Middle East between the Arab nations and Israel and a permanent settlement of the Israeli-Palestinian conflict. This plan was drafted by the United States with input from Russia, the European Union, and the United Nations. In its early stages this plan was referred to as the Quartet Peace Plan because it was written by the aforementioned four parties. The plan serves as a great outline of the terms and conditions necessary for all sides to agree to if a permanent settlement is to be achieved.

On April 30, 2003, shortly after the U.S.-led War on Iraq, the U.S. State Department released the official copy of what has become known as the "Road Map To Peace" between the Israelis and the Palestinians. This plan was consistent with and reaffirmed the contents of the Mitchell Report. This document encompasses the specifics of the Quartet Plan. The Road Map outlined three steps or phases that the Palestinian Authority and the Israeli government must each take to reach a permanent settlement. The Road Map also included a tentative timeline for implementing its provisions. The end goal of the Road Map is a permanent peace settlement between the parties that results in the acceptance of a two-state solution (Palestine and Israel living side by side) between the Israelis and Palestinians by 2005. Obviously this date has come and gone.

The Road Map also called on the leaders of the Arab world to normalize diplomatic and trade relations with Israel prior to the completion of the Road Map. A meeting of the Arab League in Beirut, Lebanon during the spring of 2002 resulted in unanimous endorsement by the Arab countries of a Saudi Arabian proposal by Crown Prince Abdullah for Arab acceptance of Israel as a neighbor living in peace and security in the context of a comprehensive peace settlement. This was obviously a very positive and historic development paving the way for future talks and peace settlements.

Although the Road Map encompassed many positive and significant measures for achieving peace, the provisions contained in the document were never fully implemented or realized. As mentioned earlier, the Quartet Plan Road Map To Peace included three phases. Phase 1, which was scheduled to occur by the end of May 2003, calls on the Palestinians to take all measures necessary to achieve an unconditional cessation of violence and terrorism against Israel and to undertake comprehensive political reform in preparation for statehood, including drafting a Palestinian Constitution that encompasses a parliamentary democratic system and to hold free, fair, and open elections for their government leaders. These reforms of the Palestinian Authority are necessary for the reasons cited earlier, namely to end the corruption and restore public confidence in the ability of the Palestinian Authority to manage its own affairs and to be a willing and trusting partner in the peace process. The Palestinian Authority was also required to issue an "unequivocal" statement reiterating Israel's right to exist in peace and security and to crack down on militants encouraging incitement of violence and terror against Israel. Israel, likewise, was called upon to take steps to normalize Palestinian life, to withdraw from areas occupied after September 28, 2000, to halt its home demolitions policy and attacks on Palestinian civilians as collective punishment, to refrain from engaging in the destruction of Palestinian infrastructure and institutions, and to affirm its commitment to the two-state vision of an independent and sovereign Palestinian state living in peace and security alongside Israel, as expressed by President Bush. This phase also called upon the Arab countries to end their financial and moral support to organizations supporting and engaging in violence and terror against Israel.

Phase II of the Road Map involved the creation of an independent Palestinian state with provisional borders and attributes of sovereignty by December 2003 after the Palestinian leadership has acted decisively against terror. The progress of Phase II was to be based upon the consensus judgment of the Quartet (United States, Russia, United Nations, and European Union) on whether the conditions are appropriate to proceed. Phase II also encompassed the normalization of relations between Israel and her Arab neighbors. This would include cooperation on issues of trade, security, arms control, sharing of resources, economic development, and refugees. Finally, Phase II would also provide for an international role, monitored by the Quartet members, in overseeing the transition.

Phase III involved a permanent status agreement and end of the Israeli-Palestinian conflict in 2004-2005. Like Phase II, progress into Phase III would be based on a consensus judgment of the Quartet parties. The beginning of this phase involved an agreement on the status of an independent Palestinian state with provisional borders in 2004 which would lead to a final, permanent status resolution in 2005 on borders, Jerusalem, refugees, settlements, and progress toward a comprehensive Middle East peace settlement between Israel and Lebanon and Israel and Syria, to be achieved as soon as possible. Phase III also required Arab state acceptance of full normal relations with Israel and security for all the nations of the region in the context of a comprehensive Arab-Israeli peace.

The reaction by Palestinians and Israelis to the Quartet Plan Road Map To Peace has been mixed. The Palestinian Authority has fully accepted the Quartet Road Map and has started to implement its provisions. This has included the appointment of Mahmoud Abbas, also known as Abu Mazen, as

Prime Minister of the Palestinian Authority as part of an internal reform and reorganization plan for the Palestinian Authority demanded by Israel and the United States as a condition for re-opening negotiations between the Israeli government and Palestinian leaders. Abbas is a highly-respected and well-educated leader in the Palestinian Authority. He is admired by many Palestinians and Israelis alike. Abbas is viewed as a moderate and is credited with being the chief architect behind the 1993 Oslo Peace Accords between Rabin and Arafat.

The Palestinian Parliament confirmed Abbas's appointment as Prime Minister on April 29, 2003. Abbas has promised to take all steps necessary to end the Intifada and terror attacks against Israel. This is hopeful news. Even so, it must be noted that even though Abbas will now be the chief negotiator for the Palestinians. Abbas also personally endorsed the Quartet Plan Road Map To Peace in May 2003. The biggest challenge facing Abbas will be to make good on his promise to end the violence and incitement against Israel and to then secure positive confidence-building measures from the Israeli government, including the halting of Israeli settlements.

The Israeli government response to the Bush-backed Quartet Plan Road Map To Peace has been even more sporadic. In January 2003, when asked to comment on the early stages of the plan, then Prime Minister Ariel Sharon responded, "Oh, the Quartet is nothing. Don't take it seriously."[2] Some progress was made on May 26, 2003 when the Israeli government approved the Quartet Plan Road Map To Peace with major conditions attached. The Israeli government approved the "steps defined by the road map" but not the entire document.[3] One of the major reservations by Israel included the right of return of up to four million Palestinian refugees to the West Bank and Gaza Strip in a newly created Palestinian state. This right of return of Palestinian refugees is scheduled to be negotiated in the third and final stage of the Quartet Peace Plan. On the same day, Ariel Sharon appeared somewhat more conciliatory and stated, "To keep 3.5 million [Palestinian] people under occupation is bad for us and them."[4] In contrast, statements such as this, if followed by appropriate action, are much more likely to facilitate positive dialogue and assist in creating the climate necessary to achieve peace.

Although the deadlines outlined earlier proposed by the Road Map have passed, the Road Map continues to exist as an important framework for resuming meaningful negotiations between Israel and the Palestinians resulting in a final status settlement between the parties.

In 2003, members of the Israeli left and Palestinian opposition leaders finalized a new draft agreement, the Geneva Initiative, which they hoped would replace the failed Oslo Accords. The Agreement was negotiated by Israeli Shahar Party leader Yossi Beilin and Palestinian activist Yasser Abd-Rabbo. Abd-Rabbo has been a longtime member of the Palestine Liberation Organization's Executive Committee and currently serves as an advisor to

Palestinian President Yasir Arafat. Abd-Rabbo played an important role in the initial negotiations leading up to the finalization of the Oslo peace Accords. Beilin is a former member of the Israeli Knesset, past Labor Party activist, and was also involved in negotiating the Oslo Peace Accords.

Not surprisingly, the Geneva Initiative was rooted in and largely resembled the Oslo Peace Accords. The Geneva Initiative allows for the following: (1) Israel withdraws to pre-1967 borders with minor alterations; (2) The division of Jerusalem with Arab neighborhoods in East Jerusalem serving as the capital of a future Palestinian state; (3) The Palestinians recognize pre-1967 Israel as a Jewish state; (4) The Palestinians agree to a demilitarized state and to prevent violence and incitement towards Israel; (5) The Palestinians would agree to a limited right of return of Palestinian refugees mostly within a new Palestinian state while others who do not return would be eligible for some financial compensation; and (6) The provisions contained in the Geneva Initiative would replace all prior agreements and United Nations Resolutions.

The major modifications from prior agreements contained in the Geneva Initiative included Israel giving up sovereignty over East Jerusalem, including the Temple Mount, Ariel, and Efrat. The Palestinians, in turn, would give up the Right of return of Palestinian refugees to Israel. Israeli Government officials, led by then-Prime Minister Ariel Sharon were quick to condemn the Geneva Initiative as did former opposition Labor Party Leader Ehud Barak. The Palestinian leadership, on the other hand, welcomed the document as a basis for final status negotiations.

In March 2007, members of the Arab League reaffirmed their support for an April 2002 Saudi proposal that offered normal Arab relations with Israel in exchange for Israel's withdrawal to its 1967 borders, the establishment of a Palestinian capital in East Jerusalem, and Israel's acknowledgement of the right of return of Palestinian refugees displaced after 1947. All 22 Arab nations have embraced the Saudi peace initiative, which has become known as the Riyadh and Beirut Declarations because the 2002 Arab League summit, where the plan was initially proposed, was held in Beirut.

Israeli leaders, including then Prime Minister Ehud Olmert, initially welcomed the Saudi proposal, but expressed reservations about the specific provisions. Former Prime Minister Ehud Barak remarked on Israel's Army Radio, "There is definitely room to introduce a comprehensive Israeli plan to counter the Saudi's plan that would be the basis for a discussion on overall peace."[5] Unfortunately, Israel's government has still not presented a plan of their own to counter the Saudi proposal as a basis for negotiations.

The West Bank remains mostly under Israeli control while the Gaza Strip is being largely administered by Hamas leaders in conjunction with Palestinian Authority officials.[6]

The West Bank, as well as Gaza, needs to be revitalized economically before meaningful peace can be achieved. As University of Texas at Austin Professor George Gavrilis notes in *Foreign Affairs*, removing Israeli checkpoints in the West Bank is crucial in helping the Palestinians improve the regional economy and attract foreign business ventures in the area.[7]

Since Israeli withdrawal from the Gaza Strip, the Quartet Nations have focused their efforts on improving conditions in Gaza and pressuring Palestinian President Mahmoud Abbas to disarm Hamas. This has produced mixed results. In instituting the Israeli settlement dismantlements in Gaza, Israel acted unilaterally and did not cooperate with Palestinian leaders. This has resulted in Abbas and Palestinian Authority leaders being placed in a weakened position among Palestinians. Educated observers note that under present conditions, a forced disarmament of Hamas would lead to civil war between Palestinians.[8]

More than 6,500 Palestinians and nearly 1,100 Israelis have been killed in fighting between 2000-2011. In addition, there are more than 11,000 Palestinians being held in Israeli jails for inciting violence against Israel.[9]

NOTES

1. Rachelle Marshall, "The Dangerous Legacy of Occupation." *The Washington Report on Middle East Affairs*, August 2007.
2. "Sharon Dismisses Quartet Peace Plan," *Associated Press*, January 19, 2003.
3. Kevin Laub, "Israel OK's Peace Plan," *Associated* Press, May 26, 2003.
4. Mark Lavie, "Sharon's Conciliatory Tone Shocks Israel's Hawks," *Associated Press*, May 27, 2003.
5. Aron Heller, "Barak: Israel Considering Saudi Plan," *Associated Press*, October 19, 2008.
6. George Gavrilis, "The Forgotten West Bank, *Foreign Affairs*, January/February 2006, 67.
7. Ibid.
8. Lally Weymouth, "A Very Fateful Step," *Newsweek*, September 19, 2005, 56.
9. Mohammed Daraghmeh, "After Losses, Palestinian Zeal For Intifadah Flongs, " *Boston Sunday Globe*, September 30, 2007, A17.

Chapter Nine

Why Oslo Failed

A Historiography

For nearly sixty years, Israelis and Palestinians have strived to make significant territorial and political gains at the expense of the other side. The primary purpose of the 1993 Oslo Peace Accords was to establish a process that would enable the Israelis and Palestinians to reach a permanent status agreement based on peace, co-existence, and mutual recognition. The Oslo Peace Accords were formally agreed to and signed in September 1993. They were the result of at least two years of behind-the-scenes talks and negotiations between the Israeli and the Palestinian leaders.

The Oslo Accords established the aim of negotiations and a framework for an interim period. It also established a time frame for free elections in the Palestinian areas of the West Bank and Gaza Strip, economic collaboration, withdrawal of Israeli troops from select areas of the West Bank and Gaza Strip, and security guarantees for Israel. It was understood that the final results of the Accords would be the creation of an independent Palestinian state. The Accords also provided for follow-up agreements to be negotiated leading up to a final status arrangement of September 2000. The Cairo Accords, Oslo B Interim Agreements, and the Wye River Memorandum were added between 1993 and 1998 in order to supplement the original Oslo Accords and to establish time frames and procedures for the implementations of its provisions.

Shortly after the Oslo Peace Accords went into effect, problems began to arise. Deterioration in negotiations and trust between both sides culminated when the final status talks held at Camp David in September 2000 proved a complete failure, which resulted in a complete breakdown in trust and negotiations between the two sides. More violence and acts of terror followed. Both the Israelis and the Palestinians blamed each other for the failures and each accused the other of failing to live up to provisions contained in the Oslo Agreements.

Conditions leading up to the final discussions deteriorated rapidly beforehand and have arguably worsened to this day. What went wrong? Why did the Oslo Accords fail to produce the intended result? What conditions are necessary to produce a final settlement? This chapter will attempt to provide answers to these questions from the point of view of historians.

There are really two schools of thought when exploring why the Oslo Accords failed to achieve the intended result of peace between Israelis and Palestinians. One interpretation holds that the provisions contained in the Oslo Accords were purposely vague and thus easily misinterpreted by each side and neither party carried out fully what was expected by the other. Another school of thought maintains that neither the right conditions, nor the right intentions, were present when the Oslo Accords were signed and that the time frame established for enactment of its provisions was unrealistic. Because of this, Israeli and Palestinian leaders manipulated the Oslo Peace Accords in order to deceive the opposing side.

FIRST SCHOOL OF THOUGHT: OSLO WAS PURPOSELY VAGUE

It can be legitimately argued that the Palestinians did not bargain skillfully when negotiating the Oslo Peace Accords, according to Professor Camille Mansour, who teaches International Relations at Paris and Versailles Universities. According to Mansour, the Palestinian negotiators at Oslo, led by the PLO, made too many unnecessary concessions and compromises at the beginning. He notes that the PLO accepted U.N. Resolution 242, which fails to directly address the fundamental issue of Palestinian statehood, without obtaining any future guarantees in return. The PLO also recognized Israel within pre-1967 boundaries without obtaining Israeli recognition of a future Palestinian state.[1]

Mansour maintains that there were two possible interpretations of Oslo that resulted from the vague and ambiguous wording of the agreements. The first reading held that the economic, political, and social components of the agreement would be shared evenly and quickly by both the Palestinians and Israelis. Thus, it was grounded in good faith. The second interpretation seemed to indicate that the Accords were a strategic military strategy designed to benefit the Israelis, who were finding it increasingly costly and difficult to maintain security in the Palestinian areas of the West Bank and Gaza Strip. This latter interpretation was also grounded in the Israeli government's conclusion that it would strictly control the security and political operations of the new Palestinian Authority [PA]. In addition, the PA, as the de-facto agent of the Israeli government, would be willing to accept whatever arrangement the Israelis offered in final status negotiations.[2]

Professor Mansour argues that a reading of the Oslo Agreement within the framework of the first interpretation would imply that Israeli settlement activities in the Palestinian-dominated areas of the West Bank and Gaza Strip would be minimized and eventually uprooted. Since this did not happen, Mansour concludes that the Israeli government intended for the second interpretation. Mansour notes that Israeli settlement expansion in the West Bank increased by almost two-thirds between 1993-2000. He adds that settlements were increasing even during the final status negotiations at Camp David in July 2000.[3] Mansour observes that the Second Palestinian Uprising following the failed 2000 negotiations served as an indication to the world community that Palestinians were going to insist on the first interpretation of the Oslo Accords and on the full application of international resolutions and mandates.[4]

In *The Oslo Accords: International Law and the Israeli-Palestinian Peace Agreements*, Law Professor Geoffrey Watson argues that both the Israelis and the negotiators for the Palestinians intended for the Oslo Peace Accords to be legally binding under international law.[5] In other words, the provisions are binding and enforceable as agreed to. This is especially problematic when you consider how vague the provisions that it contains really are. In reviewing Watson's claims in *The American Journal of International Law*, Robbie Sabel argues, in contrast that "Moreover, until the PLO or the PA satisfies the objective requirement of statehood, neither is in a position to assume most of the other international responsibilities of a state."[6] To further support his contention, Sabel adds, "Neither the PA or PLO can become a member of any intergovernmental organization open only to states."[7] Researcher Kathleen Cavanaugh from Queen's University of Belfast agrees with the assessment that the Oslo Peace Accords were vague when considering international law. According to Professor Cavanaugh, the Oslo Accords constitute an internal agreement between Israelis and Palestinians so as such are not subject to the strict standards of international law. She points out that the Oslo Declaration of Principles of 1993 were deliberately vague. This is because Article I indicates that final status negotiations will result in the implementation of U.N. Security Council Resolutions 242 and 338 while also deferring the most disputable issues of contention – Jerusalem, Israeli settlements, Palestinian refugees, borderlines, and security guarantees – were left to final status negotiations.[8] Dr. Cavanaugh thus concludes, "Therefore, while the DOP calls for the implementation of 242 and 338, which requires Israel's withdrawal from the Occupied Territories, it also allows Israel to maintain control over settlements in the West Bank, Gaza and East Jerusalem."[9] She adds, "The PA's limited legislative powers do not allow it to review matters outside of those accorded it under the interim agreements."[10]

Professor Cavanaugh also points out that the Oslo Agreements placed no restrictions on Israeli settlement activity during the transition period and also provided that all settlement issues would fall under exclusive Israeli jurisdiction during the same period.[11] She adds that although the Oslo Accords created an initial pact between Israelis and Palestinians, the vague wording "also enabled Israel to claim compliance with the Accords while violating international law."[12]

SECOND SCHOOL OF THOUGHT: OSLO WAS MANIPULATED

Sara Roy, who works as a research associate at Harvard University's Center for Middle Eastern Studies, writes that the Palestinian society and economy before Oslo, had grown to be largely dependent on Israel. After the Agreements, the conditions were not present for achieving economic, political, and social independence within the Palestinian territories. Might this help explain the acceptance of vague of key provisions wording by the Palestinian negotiators? Roy further notes that Palestinian society degenerated and became exploited by severe economic depression, social decline, and political suppression, following the Oslo Agreements of 1993.[13] Thus, it would appear that the favorable conditions were absent for achieving peace both prior to and following the signing of the Oslo Peace Accords.

University of Missouri-Columbia Political Science Professor Mkhaimar Abu Sada has compiled research data to show that the signing of the Oslo Peace Accords created many divisions among the Palestinian population. This would seem to confirm the belief that favorable conditions for achieving a lasting settlement were largely absent following the signing of the Oslo Accords. Prior to the Accords, Abu Sada writes, that the shared goals outweighed the differences among the Palestinian population.[14] Professor Abu Sada points out that Palestinian society is largely agrarian and lacks the advances of modern industry. In discussing his research encompassing his surveying of the Palestinian population, Professor Abu Sada notes, "Better educated respondents are critical of the peace negotiations and the Oslo Accords."[15] He adds, "By virtue of their education, better educated respondents have access to more information about the roots of the Palestinian-Israeli conflict and the defects of the Oslo Agreement."[16] According to Professor Abu Sada, 85% of the Palestinian population supported the Oslo Accords and the peace process as late as December 1995, but the support declined greatly following new Israeli settlement constructions the following year.[17]

Conditions had worsened by 1998 according to University of Massachusetts-Dartmouth Political Science Professor Naseer H. Aruri. Following the Oslo Peace Agreements, the Israeli government followed a policy of Palestinian home demolitions, economic restraints, collective punishment, and land expropriations.[18] Professor Aruri maintains that the supplemental 1998 Wye Memorandum agreement between Israelis and Palestinians committed the PA, under the guise of reciprocity, to new security arrangements designed to suppress Palestinian opposition to the Israeli occupation while doing away with Palestinian human rights. He argues that the 1998 Wye Memorandum was designed to address the concerns of Israelis opposed to the Oslo Agreements while also taking into account the feelings of Israelis who supported the Accords.[19] Professor Aruri points out that the Wye Memorandum required Palestinian Authority officials to suppress internal opposition to the vague Oslo Accords. It provided for Israeli redeployment from a small area of Palestinian land in the West Bank in return for new security arrangements to be guaranteed by Palestinians in addition to a promise to assist the Israeli government in fighting terror.[20]

According to Professor Aruri, the Wye Memorandum also reinterprets the Oslo Accords from the Israeli perspective. He points out that while the Oslo Accords called for Israeli military forces to be redeployed to certain military areas, the locations were not defined. The Wye Memorandum, Aruri adds, allowed these areas of redeployment to be determined solely by Israel, not mutually agreed upon.[21] Professor Aruri also writes that the Wye Memorandum contained two security requirements for the Palestinians. The first required "outlawing and combating terrorist organizations," and the second, "preventing incitement."[22] He further observes that the Wye Memorandum was structured on the presumption that the Palestinians were responsible for the deadlocks resulting from the Oslo Peace process. Aruri notes that the Wye Memorandum did not mention three scheduled Israeli troop withdrawals that failed to happen even though they were previously agreed to. On the other hand, many provisions outlined the Palestinian Authority's security obligations. All of this implies that the PA, and not the Israeli government, were largely to blame for the failures of the Oslo peace process.[23] In his final assessment of the Wye Memorandum, Professor Aruri concludes, "What is perhaps most striking about the reactions of the parties concerned was their unanimous emphasis on security – Israel's security."[24]

Clayton Swisher, a former federal criminal investigator and an associate with a Middle East consulting firm in Washington D.C. wrote a 2004 book detailing the collapse of the Oslo peace process. In *The Truth About Camp David: The Untold Story About The Collapse of the Middle East Peace Process*, Swisher substantiates the view that the Israeli government manipulated the intent of the Oslo Accords by their stated interpretation. Beginning in the Fall 1999, Israeli Prime Minister Ehud Barak kept repeating that United Nations Resolution 242, which calls on Israel to withdraw to its pre-1967 borders and was cited in Oslo and subsequent agreements, would not serve as the basis for future negotiations with the Palestinians.[25] According to Swisher, "Even Arafat himself understood that Oslo was heavily skewed toward Israel."[26] The Immediate Israeli benefit was the promise of Palestinian security and a halt to incitement against Israel. The Palestinians, on the other hand, were given limited autonomy with the formation of the new Palestinian Authority.[27]

Swisher points out that Israeli-Palestinian negotiations in 1998-1999 provided for further Israeli withdrawal from areas in the West Bank and Gaza Strip while committing the Palestinian Authority to collecting "illegal weapons" from the Palestinian police force and militants.[28] According to Swisher, when the Israelis failed to implement the scheduled troop withdrawals from Palestinian areas, the Palestinian Authority also neglected their obligations in collecting weapons and actually smuggled in more weapons for Palestinian security officials.[29] Swisher then summarizes the differences in interpretations of the provisions of the original Oslo Accords and subsequent agreements. Swisher writes, "For Israelis, this [smuggling of weapons by the Palestinians] raised concerns about the PA's overall intentions. As they [Israelis] saw it, when the PLO agreed to Oslo it had ceded the right to resist on behalf of all Palestinians."[30] Swisher continues,

> From the Palestinian perspective, the right to resist a belligerent occupation is guaranteed under the Fourth Geneva Convention's non-derogable First Additional Protocol. According to their view-a view shared by many in the international community-customary international law precludes an occupying or occupied power from signing away these rights under any circumstances.[31]

He adds, "Thus, though Oslo might have suggested otherwise, as far as many Palestinians were concerned, the right to resist occupation was never Arafat's to surrender."[32]

In *The Atlantic*, writer David Samuels argues that the actions and statements of PA Leader Yasir Arafat from 1993 to his passing in 2004 fostered a climate of mistrust between Israelis and Palestinians, which ultimately contributed to the decline of the peace process following the signing of the Oslo Peace Accords.[33] According to Samuels, Arafat was corrupt and surrounded himself with people who were the same. He points out that up to $7 billion in foreign financial assistance that was earmarked for internal improvements for the Palestinian people was stolen by the Palestinian leadership.[34] Samuels portrays Arafat as a deceitful and cunning leader who refused to accept responsibility for his personal failures and manipulated the Palestinian people for his own benefit. Instead of appropriating money to improve the infrastructure of Palestinian towns, and thus the lives of the ordinary Palestinian people after Oslo, Arafat spent large sums of money buying the loyalty of activists by awarding lucrative contracts to his supporters.[35] Samuels claims that Arafat worked to suppress opposition to his rule and treated the Palestinian people as "conquered subjects."[36] He adds that Arafat employed the strategic use of terror as a bargaining tool with Israelis.[37] The Oslo Accords, according to Samuels, created the Palestinian Authority as a central governing authority, but the leaders worked to suppress opposition and in doing so created further division among the Palestinian people. As a result, many Palestinians ignored the dictates of their leaders.[38] This begs the question, how much was Arafat trying to appease Israel by suppressing militant opposition to negotiations versus his selfish display of personal power and authority granted him under Oslo? The answer to this depends on who you ask.

Edward Said, who passed on in September 2003, was a Professor of English and Comparative Literature at Columbia University and the author of numerous articles and books on Palestinian issues. He was well-known worldwide for his tireless advocacy for Palestinian issues. Said was a member of the Palestine National Council, the umbrella organization which housed the Palestine Liberation Organization [PLO] and other organizations advocating for self-determination for the Palestinian people leading up to the Oslo Agreement. Said was one of the earliest Palestinian critics of the Oslo Accords. He opposed the Agreement from its inception. He argues that the Oslo Accords has adversely affected Palestinian aims by obstructing Palestinian efforts for self-determination in the eyes of the world community.[39] Said claims that Palestinians have simply "lost the will to resist."[40] He concluded that the Oslo Accords failed to directly address the most fundamental and pressing concerns of the Palestinian people.

In *From Oslo To Iraq: Essays*, Professor Said blames the Israelis for the failures of Oslo. He claims that continued Israeli settlement expansion, failure to cede real power to Palestinian leaders, refusal to address the status of Jerusalem, and opposition to negotiating a right of return for Palestinian refugees rendered the Oslo Accords ineffective from the beginning.[41] Thus, the Oslo Accords as viewed by Israeli leaders since 1994 was a manipulation tool to ensure security for Israel and control the Palestinian population. Said proposes a solution that amounts to a radical departure from the goals of most other Palestinian and Israeli policy-makers. Instead of complete separation leading to a two-state solution, Said advocates the creation of a single secular nation in which Israelis and Palestinians both reside under democratic governance with social and political equality.[42]

Baylis Thomas is a psychologist who has taught at Yeshiva University/ Albert Einstein College of Medicine. His book, *How Israel Was Won*, was compiled as a research project that encompassed the work of three history professors, a sociologist, and an English professor, in addition to himself. According to Thomas, Prime Minister Yitzak Rabin decided to propose the Oslo Peace Accords initially to enhance Israel's security by utilizing the PLO to police Palestinian militant groups. Since Arafat was weak and presiding over a divided PLO, Rabin saw an opportunity to utilize Arafat to Israel's advantage.[43] Thomas writes, "Rabin gave to Arafat recognition that the PLO represented the Palestinian people with whom Israel would negotiate. That is Arafat recognized both the Jewish state and its right to security while Rabin recognized Arafat as an agent for a collection of people without a state or a similar right to security."[44] He adds, "Ignored outright was the Palestinian state declared five years earlier and recognized by over 100 counties – a nullity in the Accords."[45]

Thomas argues that the most significant criticism of the Oslo Accords encompassed Arafat's promise of peace and security for Israel. Thomas comments, "This commitment made him [Arafat] responsible for Palestinian terrorism, future intifadas or other violence directed at Israelis. Israel assumed no parallel responsibility for IDF [Israeli Defense Forces] or settler violence directed at Palestinians."[46] He adds, "Moreover, Arafat's pledge to end violence set him squarely against Hamas and Islamic Jihad, thereby creating conditions for a potential civil war within the Palestinian community."[47] Thomas claims that the conditions created by the Oslo Peace Accords had predictable consequences of failure. In other words, Arafat was backed into and accepted what world amount to a no-win situation. He asks, "What was Rabin's ultimate goal in signing the Oslo Accords?"[48] Thomas concludes that Rabin's goals likely involved separating Palestinian communities into dozens of self-rule areas, but within Israeli jurisdiction. He notes that some Palestinian leaders saw what was coming early on. He points out that early critics of the Oslo Accords, including Palestine National Council Member Edward Said, realized that the Oslo Accords failed to directly address Palestinian sovereignty over the West Bank and Gaza Strip even though it allowed for some Palestinian autonomy and self-rule.[49] Later on, Thomas argues that Israeli Prime Minister Benjamin Netanyahu was committed to eroding the Oslo Agreements and the peace process itself.

Sociology Professor Baruch Kimmerling from the University of Toronto has reached similar findings and conclusions as those articulated by Baylis Thomas. Kimmerling claims that Israeli Prime Minister Yitzhak Rabin embarked on the Oslo peace process after reaching the realization that Palestinian protests to Israeli occupation could not be subdued militarily.[50] Kimmerling notes in agreement with earlier assessments that the Palestinian people and their leaders were divided and skeptical about the Oslo Accords from their inception. He argues that the mainstream Palestinian leadership viewed the Oslo Accords as a minimal and temporary arrangement that would lead to a much broader agreement resulting in the eventual creation of a Palestinian state.[51]

Following the signing of the Oslo Accords, Kimmerling claims Arafat sought to control Palestinian opposition groups by dividing and subduing them through favors and government appointments. He adds that the majority of Palestinians realized very little social, economic, or military improvements following the signing of the Oslo Accords. This only served to increase tension and discontent among the Palestinian people and resulted in a higher crime rate. Once formed, Kimmerling says, the Palestinian Authority failed to properly integrate Palestinian charity and voluntary associations into the new Palestinian government or include them fully into Palestinian society.[52] Kimmerling also maintains that diplomatic relations and trust between the Palestinians and Israelis deteriorated during the leadership of Likud Party Prime Minister Benjamin Netanyahu from 1996-1999 due to his government's open hostility towards the Palestinians and the Oslo Accords.[53] According to Kimmerling, the Palestinians interpreted the 1996 election of Netanyahu as the Israeli majority's rejection of the Oslo Peace Accords.[54]

Kimmerling claims that Netanyahu's successor, Prime Minister Ehud Barak cooperated with right-wing religious parties opposed to the peace process. In addition, Kimmerling maintains that Barak "genuinely believed that Israel was strong enough to coerce the Palestinians into accepting an agreement based on his own conditions."[55] He points out that Barak had objected to the Oslo Accords even as Israeli Chief of Staff under Yitzak Rabin's premiership.[56] Kimmerling adds that Barak actually believed that he could achieve an agreement that resulted in the creation of a limited and demilitarized Palestinian state without an Israeli withdrawal to 1967 borders. Kimmerling further argues that Arafat had good reason to distrust Barak and have initial reservations about participating in the final status negotiations since Barak had failed to live up to the provisions of previous agreements by ending Israeli settlements and releasing Palestinian prisoners held in Israeli jails.[57]

Kimmerling writes that the Palestinian negotiators believed that they were undertaking significant concessions by giving up 78 percent of historic Palestine as a precursor to a final status agreement with Israel.[58] He adds that during the final status talks, Arafat also offered to compromise between 8 and 10 percent of the occupied Palestinian territory. Kimmerling also notes that the political climate following the attacks of September 11, 2001 created one in favor of Israel and had adverse effects on the Palestinians in their quest for an independent state.[59] Finally, Kimmerling maintains that the goal of then Israeli Prime Minister Ariel Sharon was to reduce Palestinian expectations, destroy their resistance, isolate them politically, and force them to accept a final agreement imposed by the Israeli government.[60] Kimmerling concludes that the concessions being made by Sharon were designed to buy time in order to ultimately destroy the Palestinian Authority.[61]

In her book, *Israel/Palestine: How To End The War of 1948*, author and Hebrew University Professor Tanya Reinhart confirms Kimmerling's arguments regarding Palestinian feelings on land concessions during negotiations. She claims that the Palestinians believed that they were giving up 80 percent of their historic nation, where they once lived to claim the Gaza Strip and West Bank as the only area for a future Palestinian state.[62] Amira Haas, an Israeli correspondent for the Israeli newspaper *Ha'aretz*, who began to live in the Gaza Strip in 1993, reported that since Oslo Israel has enlarged and doubled the number of settlers in the West Bank. She argues that the Oslo Agreements "upheld Israel's position as a sovereign power" and denied Palestinians to even have undeveloped land in the occupied territories for future Jewish development. Haas maintains that this building of settlements takes away from the political rights of Palestinians and further instigates the conflict with Israel.[63]

Researchers Anita Miller, Jordan Miller, and Sigalit Zetouni compiled a 2002 historical biography titled *Sharon: Israel's Warrior Politician*. The work is written for both a general and an academic audience. It is written in a narrative form of a story. The authors divide the book into 84 sections, which cover in detail the actions and accomplishments of former Israeli Prime Minister Ariel Sharon from his early years through his election as Prime Minister in 2001. They point out that Sharon had railed against the Oslo Agreements and in doing so called Rabin a traitor. Sharon had promised to dismantle the Accords if his Likud Party gained power. The authors maintain that Sharon and the Israeli right-wing viewed the Oslo Accords as a dangerous sell-out that would result in the creation of a Palestinian terror state.[64]

The Oslo Peace Accords of 1993 and the subsequent agreements constituted the closest attempt and effort at achieving peace between the Palestinians and Israelis. In considering the intentions of the two schools of thought outlined earlier regarding the Oslo Peace Accords, most of the published literature seems to reveal that the second school of thought is most plausible and accepted. The fact that the provisions contained in the original Oslo Peace Accords were vague and ambiguous remains largely undisputed. This allowed the politicians and leaders of both sides, but especially the Israelis who have experienced four prime ministers since 1993, to interpret the Accords to correspond with their own political wants and agendas. The biggest failure of the Oslo Peace Accords may lie in the absence of both sides to agree to more specific language, incorporate a mechanism for effectively resolving the most disputed issues of contention in a fair and concise manner, and establishing realistic timetables for the implementation of the provisions.

NOTES

1. Camille Mansour, "Israel's Colonial Impasse," *Journal of Palestine Studies*, (Summer 2001, vol. 30 no. 4): 87.
2. Ibid, 84.
3. Ibid, 84-85.
4. Ibid, 87.
5. Geoffrey Watson. *The Oslo Accords: International Law and the Israeli-Palestinian Peace Agreements* (New York: Oxford University Press, 2000), 250.

6. Robbie Sabel, Book Review For *The Oslo Accords: International Law and the Palestinian-Israeli Peace Agreements*, *The American Journal of International Law*, (January 2001, vol. 95 no. 2): 251.
7. Ibid, 251.
8. Kathleen Cavanaugh, "The Cost of Peace: Assessing the Palestinian-Israeli Accords," *Middle East Report*, (Summer 1999, no. 211): 10-12 + 15.
9. Ibid, 11.
10. Ibid, 11.
11. Ibid, 11.
12. Ibid, 12.
13. Sara Roy, "Dedevelopment Revisited: Palestinian Economy and Society Since Oslo, *Journal of Palestine Studies*, (Spring 1999, vol. 28 no. 3): 64-82.
14. Mkhaimar S. Abu Sada, "Party Identification and Political Attitudes In An Emerging Democracy: A Summary," *American Journal of Political Science*, (April 1998, vol. 42 no. 2): 712-715.
15. Ibid, 713.
16. Ibid, 713.
17. Ibid, 715.
18. Naseer H. Aruri, "The Wye Memorandum: Netanyahu's Oslo and Unreciprocal Reciprocity," *Journal of Palestine Studies*, (Winter 1999, vol. 28 no. 2): 25.
19. Ibid, 17-28.
20. Ibid, 19-22.
21. Ibid, 20.
22. Ibid, 21.
23. Ibid, 22.
24. Ibid, 24.
25. Swisher, Clayton. *The Truth About Camp David: The Untold Story About The Collapse of the Middle East Peace Process* (New York: Nation Books, 2004), 167-169.
26. Ibid, 137.
27. Ibid, 137-138.
28. Ibid, 142.
29. Ibid.
30. Ibid.
31. Ibid, 142-143.
32. Ibid, 143.
33. David Samuels, "How Yasir Arafat Destroyed Palestine," *The Atlantic*, September 1995, 61.
34. Ibid, 64.
35. Ibid, 65-67.
36. Ibid, 74.
37. Ibid, 77.
38. Ibid, 91.
39. Said, Edward. *Peace and its Discontents: Essays on Palestine in the Middle East Peace Process* (New York: Vintage Books, 1996): 57.
40. Ibid, xxv.
41. Said, Edward. *From Oslo To Iraq: Essays* (New York: Vintage Books, 2004), 5-6.
42. Ibid, 287.
43. Baylis Thomas. *How Israel was Won: A Concise History of the Arab-Israeli Conflict* (New York: Lexington Books, 1999), 264.
44. Ibid, 266.
45. Ibid.
46. Ibid, 267.
47. Ibid.
48. Ibid.
49. Ibid, 264-268.

50. Baruch Kimmerling. *Politicide: Ariel Sharon's War Against The Palestinians* (New York: Verso, 2003), 108.
51. Ibid, 112-115.
52. Ibid, 122-123.
53. Ibid, 125.
54. Ibid, 134-135.
55. Ibid, 127.
56. Ibid.
57. Ibid, 128-129.
58. Ibid, 134.
59. Ibid, 206.
60. Ibid, 211.
61. Ibid, 208.
62. Reinhart, Tanya. *Israel/Palestine: How To End The War of 1948* (New York: Seven Stories Press, 2002), 14.
63. Amira Haas. *Drinking the Sea At Gaza: Days and Nights In A Land Under Seige* (New York: Owl Books, 2000), 348-349.
64. Anita Miller, Jordan Miller, and Sigalit Zetouni. *Sharon: Israel's Warrior Politician* (Chicago: Academy Chicago Publishers & Olive Publishing, 2002), 188-190.

Chapter Ten

The U.S. as Mediator

Is Peace Possible?

Former U.S. President John F. Kennedy once observed, "Those who make peaceful change impossible make violent change inevitable." If we are to prevent catastrophe in an area of the world vital to our national interests, the United States has a very important diplomatic and political role to play to ensure peace and stability prevail in the Middle East.

King Abdullah II of Jordan told a Joint Session of the U.S. Congress in March 2007 that there could be no resolve to any other problems in the Middle East without significant progress toward an Israeli-Palestinian peace settlement. These are among the truest words ever spoken.

Council on Foreign Relations President Richard Haas maintains that Israel and Iran will yield tremendous power in the Middle East in the years to come. The former country possesses nuclear weapons while the latter seeks them and holds impressive influence over the Islamic fundamentalist groups Hamas and Hezbollah.[1]

In an editorial for the *Chicago Tribune* on May 9, 2010, University of Chicago Professor of Political Science John Mearsheimer observed that there are four possible outcomes regarding Israel and the Palestinians: 1) A two-state solution that allows for an independent Palestinian nation-state in the West Bank and Gaza Strip with a shared or divided Jerusalem; 2) Israel retains control over the West Bank and Gaza Strip, but grants the Palestinian population full democratic rights in a binational state, which would eventually lead to the demise of Israel as a Jewish state since the Palestinian population will eventually outnumber the Jewish population residing in Israel; 3) Israel retains the West Bank and Gaza Strip, but expels Palestinians from these territories through ethnic cleansing; or 4) Israel tightens its control over the West Bank and Gaza Strip, but permits limited Palestinian self-rule in the territories. Mearsheimer concludes, "The two-state solution is the best of these alternatives, but most Israelis are opposed to making the sacrifices that would be necessary to create a viable Palestinian state."[2] This is certainly a pessimistic view. I believe that a majority of Israelis do favor a peace settlement resulting in a two-state solution. Unfortunately, although the Palestinians and much of the world would like to see the first outcome encompassing a two-state solution come to fruition, most of Israel's Likud Party leadership seems content on maintaining the fourth option of allowing only limited Palestinian self-rule in the territories.

The Arab Spring that the world witnessed beginning in December 2010 offers new hope for peace and transformation in all of the Middle East. The young guard rose up against tyrannical rulers in Egypt, Tunisia, Algeria, and Libya. Similar events are now unfolding in Yemen, Iran, and Syria as well. Although Islamic fundamentalist movements are well-organized in these nations, many are calling for democratic reforms and liberalization as well. The Palestinians are among the most educated of the Arab peoples and have been among the most receptive towards democracy.

The Gaza Strip, which consists of a 140-square mile strip of land, contains approximately 1.5 million Palestinian residents while the West Bank has about 2.6 million Palestinian residents. Approximately 177,000 Jewish settlers reside in Palestinian East Jerusalem and about 187,000 additional Israeli settlers reside in the West Bank. In 2007, about 47.6% of the Palestinian population was 14 years old or younger in Gaza while about 42.4% were the same in the West Bank.[3]

Approximately 63.7% of Palestinians live below the poverty line in the Gaza Strip while 45.7% live below poverty in the West Bank. The largest percentage of Palestinian workers (70% in Gaza and 55% in the West Bank) are employed in service jobs. The next largest number of workers (18% in Gaza and 29% in the West Bank) are employed in industry. The smallest number of workers (12% in Gaza and 16% in the West Bank) make their living as farmers or in the agricultural sector.[4] The unemployment rate in both the West Bank and Gaza exceeds 25%.

100 percent of Gaza's gas supplies, 60 percent of its electricity, and 40 percent of its water comes from Israel.[5] The Gaza Strip, which borders only Israel and Egypt as well as the Mediterranean Sea, has been almost completely sealed off by Israel.

When asked whether or not he was optimistic about Israel's future, former U.S. President Jimmy Carter stated bluntly, "No, I'm not. The U.S. has the least influence in the Middle East now than it's had since Israel was formed. We are totally immune from any form of influence from the Palestinians or the Arab world."[6] President Carter went on to say, "We are completely in bed with the Israelis, who are persecuting the Palestinians horribly, and this is contrary, I think, to the best interest of Israel."[7] Certainly, American policy needs to change in the region for a meaningful peace settlement to be viable.

There is certainly reason to be optimistic about peace. Approximately 70% of Israelis, according to a poll conducted by the Truman institute for the Advancement of Peace, in Jerusalem favor a two-state solution to the Israeli-Palestinian dispute resulting in an independent Palestinian nation-state.[8] Writing in *Foreign Affairs* magazine, Yossi Klein Halevi, a Fellow at the Shalom Hartman Institute in Jerusalem, maintains, "Centrist Israelis realize that the Jewish state cannot indefinitely remain both an occupier and a member in good standing of the Western club of liberal democracies."[9]

The choice that Israel faces is to negotiate a two-state solution that allows for the creation of an independent Palestinian state while maintaining Israel's identity as a Jewish state, or eventually be forced to incorporate the Palestinian population into the political system of a Greater Israel and risk losing that nation's standing as a Jewish majority nation-state. Former Israeli Prime Minister Ehud Barak observed in February 2010, "As long as between the Jordan and the Sea there is only one political entity, named Israel, it will either end up being non-Jewish or non-democratic...If the Palestinians vote in elections, it is a binational state; and if they don't vote, it is an apartheid state."[10]

On the other hand, with the exception of minor occasional skirmishes, things have been relatively quiet in Israel since the completion of the West Bank barrier wall. Writing for *Time* magazine, reporter Karl Vick observes that "without a single suicide bombing on their territory, with the economy robust and with souls a trifle weary of having to handle big elemental thoughts, the Israeli public prefers to explore such satisfactions as might be available from the private sphere, in a land first imagined as a utopia."[11] Vick further cites a 2007 survey of Israeli Jews where they described themselves as happy.[12] The fact remains that Israel avoided the economic decisions and excess debt that plunged the United States and Europe into recession. Vick remarks, "All this has combined to make the Palestinian question distant from the minds of many Israelis."[13] The Wall constructed by the Israelis, Vick notes, has not only prevented suicide bombers from crossing the border, but it has sealed off the Palestinians in the West Bank from the Israel. With the Wall now in place, Vick observes that "An Israeli Jew can easily pass an entire lifetime" without meeting a Palestinian.[14]

The fact remains that the Palestinian population is growing significantly and stands to outpace the growth of the Jewish population of Israel in the next 30 years. Palestinian women in the West Bank are conceiving an average of 5.5 children each while Palestinian women in Gaza are conceiving on average 6.6 children. By 2030, it is estimated that there will be approximately 2 million Palestinians living in Israel and an additional 7 million residing in the West Bank and Gaza. By 2050, there will be approximately 3 million Palestinians living in Israel and 12 million in Gaza. The Palestinian population in neighboring Jordan, which already encompasses 60% of the population in that nation, will also grow significantly.[15] In contrast, the Jewish population of Israel in 2011 stands at 7 million. According to Israel's Ministry of Foreign Affairs, the Jewish population is expected to increase to only between 8.2 and 9 million people in 2020.[16] It is estimated that 11.2 million people will reside in Israel by 2050.[17] In writing for *Time* magazine, reporter Tim McGirk observed, "This tectonic shift in demographics is what scared even hawkish Israelis like former Prime Minister Ariel Sharon into abandoning the biblical dreams of a Greater Israel stretching from the Jordan River to the Mediterranean."[18] Former Israeli Prime Minister Ehud Olmert commented, "If we are determined to preserve the Jewish and democratic character of Israel, we must inevitably relinquish, with great pain, parts of our homeland."[19]

McGirk concludes, "In other words, if Israelis cling to the West Bank and Gaza, as many religious Zionists insist, Jews will find themselves a shrinking minority in their own state."[20] The Arabs and Palestinians are well aware of this fact also. Tim McGirk further notes, "A few bold Arab intellectuals are saying Palestinians should abandon the idea of a two-state solution and just wait until they outnumber the Jews."[21]

There is no question that U.S. President Barack Obama and current Israeli Prime Minister Benjamin Netanyahu loathe one another. Secretary of State Hillary Clinton, like her husband the former President Bill Clinton, also is not a fan of Netanyahu. President Obama has been vocal in his support for the dismantlement of Israeli settlements in the West Bank, the creation of an independent Palestinian state in the Gaza Strip and West Bank, and a return to pre-1967 borders for Israel. These measures have met strong opposition from Netanyahu, who is a Likud Party hard-liner in Israel.

Although succumbing to pressure, Netanyahu has stated that he supports a two-state solution, he envisions a much smaller and less viable Palestinian state. The Likud Party platform clearly rejects the creation of a Palestinian state in the West Bank. Former Obama Chief of Staff Rahm Emanuel, an Israeli citizen who had served as a member of the Israeli Defense Forces during the first Gulf War, warned that if the United States did not pressure Netanyahu "hard and clear and early" regarding territorial concessions in the West Bank and East Jerusalem that Netanyahu would never make any concessions during negotiations.[22] Netanyahu stated in 2010, "Jerusalem is the eternal capital of the Jewish people, a city reunified so as never again to be divided."[23]

President Obama should be commended for applying pressure to Israel's government to move forward with meaningful peace initiatives. *Time* magazine reports,

> He [Obama] asked Netanyahu to do something no other Israeli Prime Minister had done: stop the appropriation of Arab land in east Jerusalem by Jewish activists. Palestinians, who claim east Jerusalem as their capital, had made that a precondition for peace talks with Israel, but Netanyahu, who had formed his right-wing government six weeks earlier on a platform of opposing Palestinian statehood, would have none of it.[24]

In a visit to Cairo, Egypt on June 4, 2009, President Obama stated, "The United States does not accept the legitimacy of continued Israeli settlements. This construction violates previous agreements and undermines efforts to achieve peace. It is time for these settlements to stop."[25] Secretary of State Hillary Clinton has also echoed these sentiments. When addressing the American-Israeli Political Action Committee [AIPAC] on March 22, 2009, Secretary of State Clinton stated, "And yes, I underscored the longstanding American policy that does not accept the legitimacy of continued settlements."[26]

Since being elected Prime Minister in 2009, Benjamin Netanyahu has worked to expand Israeli settlements in the West Bank and Arab East Jerusalem and has even encouraged illegal Israeli settlements to be constructed in Palestinian lands, which have displaced thousands of Palestinian civilians.[27] Since the signing of the Oslo Accords in 1993 up until 2011, Israeli settlements in the West Bank have more than tripled. There are over 300,000 Israeli settlers living in the West Bank today compared with just 100,000 in 1993.[28] It has been reported that 121 settlements and 100 outposts in the West Bank now control over 42 percent of that territory.[29]

In November 2010, Israeli lawmakers, with the support of Netanyahu, passed a bill that would require a two-thirds Knesset majority or approval by the Israeli public in a national referendum to relinquish any territory to the Palestinians, including parts of East Jerusalem, or the Golan Heights to Syria. Netanyahu remarked, following the bill's passage, "Any peace agreement requires national agreement and the bill promises that."[30] Chief Palestinian negotiator Saeb Erekat responded, "With the passage of this bill, the Israeli leadership, yet again, is making a mockery of international law."[31] Erekat added, "Ending the occupation of our land is not and cannot be dependent on any sort of referendum."[32] Israel's Deputy Prime Minister Moshe Ya'alon stated in 2011, "Our intention is to leave the situation as it is: autonomous management of civil affairs. If they [the Palestinians] want to call it a state let them call it that. If they want to call it an empire, by all means. We intend to keep what exists now."[33] This statement by a top Israeli official is certainly indicative of what the Netanyahu government intends to do. To further complicate matters, Netanyahu forged an alliance between his far-right Likud Party and the center-right Kadima Party, led by Shaul Mofaz, in early May 2012. These two parties now collectively control approximately 120 seats in the 196-member Knesset parliament in Israel. This further consolidates Netanyahu's power and hold over the Israeli government. In the absence of some extraordinary change, the Netanyahu government does not plan to address the Israeli-Palestinian conflict nor work to create a meaningful two-state solution. In order for this to happen real and tremendous pressure must be applied to Israel by the United States and the rest of the international community to negotiate a settlement that serves the best interests of both the Palestinians and the Israelis.

In January 2011, Britain's *Guardian* newspaper and the Qatar-based *Al Jazeera* news organization reported that they had acquired more than 1,600 pages of confidential Palestinian documents that revealed a desperate attempt by Palestinian Authority leaders, led by Mahmoud Abbas, to create a peace deal with Israel that would have ceded the rights of hundreds of thousands of Palestinian refugees displaced and forced to relocate to refugee camps in Lebanon, Syria, and Jordan, as well as the West Bank and Gaza after losing their homes in Israel in 1948 from ever returning to Israel or even receiving compensation for the loss of their possessions. The Papers also showed that Abbas was willing to make major concessions on East Jerusalem and Israeli settlements situated in the West Bank, including illegal outposts.[34] This revelation seriously damaged the credibility of Abbas and Fatah leaders among the Palestinian population. Senior Editor of *Time* magazine, Tony Karon commented of "the Israelis being unimpressed no matter how willing the Palestinian negotiators are to concede rights that they enjoy under international law."[35] Karon noted further that it was the "sense of the slim offerings available at the negotiating table that have prompted even many leaders in Abbas' own Fatah movement to urge him to break with the U.S.-led process and adopt strategies to pressure Israel."[36] Finally, Karon observed that the Abbas concessions, which were obviously rooted in desperation for a peace agreement, "would be widely greeted by Palestinians as a betrayal."[37]

The fact remains that when Israel was created as a nation-state in 1948, more than 700,000 Palestinians were forcibly removed from their land. This fact needs to be acknowledged and resolved in order for any settlement to be viable. To make matters worse and even more complicated, in February 2011, the Obama Administration vetoed a unanimous resolution by the United Nations Security Council condemning Israeli West Bank settlements as violating international law.

According to *The New York Times*, the rivalry between the Fatah and Hamas factions since 2006 has "blocked any real hope of Palestinian statehood."[38] On May 4, 2011, Fatah and Hamas ended their four-year division and signed an agreement in Cairo, Egypt to form an interim government consisting of Hamas and Fatah members and to hold free parliamentary and Presidential elections later in 2012. As part of the agreement, all parties agreed to support an unofficial truce with Israel without preconditions. Instead of welcoming these developments as a step towards advancing the peace process, Israeli Prime Minister Benjamin Netanyahu called it "a great victory for terrorists."[39] In addition, the Obama Administration vowed to cut all aid and assistance to the Palestinian Authority. The bottom line is that for meaningful dialogue resulting in a permanent peace settlement to take place all concerned parties, including Hamas, need to be involved. Since the hardline government of Netanyahu has refused to make any meaningful concessions and has worked to isolate and divide the Palestinian factions further, it is a good development for these factions to join together an form a coalition that allows for free and democratic elections, ends attacks against Israel, and works to promote meaningful dialogue leading to a lasting peace settlement. Israel, the United States, and many European nations consider Hamas to be a terrorist organization and have stated that they would not work with a Palestinian government that includes Hamas members.[40]

Negotiations between Israel and the Palestinians have been intermittent since the Oslo Accords broke down at Camp David in 2000. The Palestinians demand an end to Israeli settlements in the West Bank and Israel's acceptance of the 1967 borders as preconditions to resuming talks. Israel is demanding that there be no pre-conditions on Israel for talks to resume and that Hamas and the Palestinian Authority recognize Israel as a Jewish state in order for further talks to take place. In 2010, Palestinian President Mahmoud Abbas remarked, "We have said that the borders need to be on a 1967 basis, with agreement on land swaps equal in value and size, and we gave our vision regarding security, which was agreed on previously, in Olmert's days."[41] Israel's Prime Minister Benjamin Netanyahu has stated, "Peace will be achieved only through direct talks."[42] I could not agree more.

Rachelle Marshall, a free-lance writer and member of A Jewish Voice For Peace, writes, "A major obstacle to the success of the peace talks is that Abbas cannot speak for a united Palestinian people."[43] Marshall adds, "Since any agreement he signs will undoubtedly require cooperation from Hamas, logic suggests that its representatives be included in the talks."[44] Ahmed Yousef, who serves as political advisor to Hamas Prime Minister Ismail Haniyeh, proposed in an op-ed piece for *The New York Times* in 2007 a 10-year cease-fire "to create an atmosphere of calm in which we can resolve our differences."[45] This is certainly a welcome development.

Time Magazine's Tim McGirk writes, "Israel's leaders need to recognize that if Hamas cannot be beaten militarily, then it must be engaged politically."[46] He adds, "That means accepting the idea of dealing with some kind of Palestinian unity government that includes Hamas."[47] McGirk concludes, "A coalition between Abbas and Hamas is essential for the future of a Palestinian state and for moderating Hamas' extremism."[48] I could not agree more. Hamas is going to have to recognize Israel as a Jewish state and eliminate charter language calling for Israel's destruction as part of a permanent peace settlement.

Martin Indyk, former U.S. ambassador to Israel maintains that U.S. President Barack Obama is well positioned to help facilitate a permanent peace settlement between Israel and the Palestinians using diplomatic options. Indyk has stated,

> He [Obama] will need to announce a series of mechanisms for achieving it, including: resumption of Israeli-Palestinian final status negotiations, rebuilding of the West Bank and Gaza Strip economies and PA security capabilities, initiation of U.S.-sponsored direct negotiations between Israel and Syria, and operationalizing the Arab League peace initiative.[49]

Edward Said was a Professor of English and Comparative Literature at Columbia University before he passed away in 2003. Said, whose views on the Oslo Peace Accords were discussed earlier, was an Episcopalian Christian Palestinian who authored more than twenty books and became a recognized authority in the Israeli-Palestinian Conflict. He was an early opponent of the Oslo Accords. Following the signing of the Oslo Peace accords, Said became a firm advocate of a single, secular state for both Israelis and Palestinians. Said points out that the Israeli government controls a crucial water supply essential to Palestinians. Said writes, "In fact, Israel controls all the water supply in the Occupied Territories, uses 80 percent of it for personal use of its Jewish citizens, rationing the rest for the Palestinian population: this issue was never seriously negotiated during the Oslo peace process."[50] An agreement regarding water usage will certainly need to be resolved in final-status negotiations.

NOTES

1. Richard Haas, "The New Middle East." *Foreign Affairs*, November/December 2006, 11.
2. John J. Mearsheimer, "Israel's Fated Bleak Future." *The Washington Report on Middle East Affairs*, July 2010, 14.
3. Tim McGirk, "How To Deal With Hamas," *Time*, July 2, 2007, 30.
4. Ibid; 30.
5. Ibid; 32.
6. Belinda Luscombe, "10 Questions," *Time* January 30, 2012.
7. Ibid.
8. Yossi Klein Halevi, "Can The Center Hold? Understanding Israel's Pragmatic Majority." *Foreign Affairs*, January/February 2012, 168.
9. Ibid.
10. Sasha Polakow-Suransky. "Middle East Plan B." *Boston Sunday Globe*, May 16, 2010, k12.
11. Karl Vick, "The Good Life And Its Dangers," *Time*, September 13, 2010, 38.
12. Ibid; 39.
13. Ibid.
14. Ibid; 40.

15. Patrick J. Buchanan. *The Death of the West* (New York: St. Martin's Griffin, 2002), 116-117.
16. Jewish Ministry of Foreign Affairs. http://www.mfa.gov.il/MFA/Government/Communiques/1999/Israel-s%20%20Population%20%2062%20Million%20%20at%20%20Millennium%20-
17. Evgenia Bystrov, MA, and Arnon Soffer, PhD, "Israel: Demography and Density 2007-2020," Reuven Chaikin Chair in Geostrategy University of Haifa, www.haifa.ac.il, May 2008.
18. Tim McGirk, "Can Israel Survive?" *Time,* January 19, 2009, 29.
19. Ibid.
20. Ibid.
21. Ibid.
22. Massimo Calabresi, "Bibi and Barack," *Time,* June 7, 2010, 29.
23. Ibid.
24. Ibid.
25. "Statements from U.S. Government Officials Concerning Israeli Settlements." Churches For Middle East Peace. http://www.cmep.org/content/us-statements-israeli-settlements_short
26. Ibid.
27. Rachelle Marshall, "Palestinians Unite and Move Toward Statehood," *The Washington Report on Middle East Affairs*, July 2011, 11.
28. Sasha Polakow-Suransky, "Middle East Plan B." *Boston Sunday Globe*, May 16, 2010, K1.
29. Rachelle Marshall, "Palestinians Reject A Compromise That Means 'Surrender,'" *The Washington Report on Middle East Affairs*, December 2010, 9.
30. Josef Federman, "Israel Adopts Referendum Bill That Could Hinder Peace Effort," *Associated Press*, November 23, 2010.
31. Ibid.
32. Ibid.
33. Rachelle Marshall, "Palestinians Unite and Move Toward Statehood," 11.
34. Tony Karon, "The Palestine Papers: Final Nail in the Coffin of the Peace Process?" http://news.yahoo.com/s/time/08599204405100/print
35. Ibid.
36. Ibid.
37. Ibid.
38. "Abbas, Hamas Leaders Hold Reconciliation Talks," *The New York Times*, March 26, 2011.
39. Rachelle Marshall, "Palestinians Unite and Move Toward Statehood," *The Washington Report on Middle East Affairs*, July 2011, 11.
40. Karin Laub and Mohammed Daraghmeh, "Palestinians Move Toward End of Political Rift," *Associated Press*, February 6, 2012.
41. Mohammed Daraghmeh, "Abbas: Israel Must Accept Previous Borders," *Associated Press*, July 18, 2010.
42. Glenn Kessler, "Impasse In Mideast Negotiations Threatens To Become Permanent," *Washington Post*, October 25, 2010.
43. Rachelle Marshall, "Peace Talks and Troop Withdrawals, But No Peace In Sight," *The Washington Report on Middle East Affairs*, November 2010, 9.
44. Ibid.
45. Ibid.
46. Tim McGirk, "Can Israel Survive?" *Time,* January 19, 2009, 29.
47. Ibid.
48. Ibid.
49. Martin Indyk, "Obama's Options," *Time*, January 19, 2009, 31.
50. Edward Said. *From Oslo To Iraq* (New York: Vintage Books, 2004), 5.

Conclusion

The assassination of Prime Minister Yitzhak Rabin in 1994 and the subsequent events that followed marked the decline of the Israeli-Palestinian peace process and hopes for a lasting and comprehensive settlement between Israelis and Palestinians. Since the signing of the Oslo Accords, many Palestinians believe that they have been betrayed by Israel's leaders since Rabin's assassination, while many Israelis have been angered by the failure of Palestinian Authority leaders to prevent incitement and halt terrorism against Israel. Since Rabin's assassination, both the Israeli government and the Palestinian Authority have breached provisions of the Oslo Accords. The Palestinians failed to halt incitements against Israel, refused to confiscate illegal firearms from Palestinian police and militants, and engaged in corrupt internal government practices.

The age old conflict between the Israelis and the Palestinians is really a tragic tale of two peoples. Countless Israelis and Palestinian Arabs have lost their lives in conflict for causes they truly believed in. Many more have been killed or seriously injured because they just happened to be in the wrong place at the wrong time. I believe that a lasting peace agreement between both sides that guarantees the security of Israel, while acknowledging the right of self-determination and statehood by the Palestinians, is in the best interests of both sides as well as in the interests of the world community.

The Oslo Accords attempted to address the fundamental issues of contention between the two sides. The Oslo Agreements established a framework for resolving the elements of dispute between the Palestinians and Israelis. First, Oslo allowed for mutual recognition between Israel and the Palestine Liberation Organization, which would become the Palestinian Authority. Next, the Accords allowed for limited self-government for the Palestinians in the West Bank and Gaza Strip under the direction of the new Palestinian

Authority and Israeli troop withdrawals. Finally, the Oslo Accords established a foundation in which future negotiations could take place leading to an agreement on the following issues: 1) An independent state for the Palestinians; 2) Agreement on the status of Jerusalem; 3) The return of Palestinian refugees; 4) Security for Israel and a Palestinian police force; and 5) Diplomatic relations and cooperation between the Palestinian Authority and Israel. The Accords also recognized United Nations Resolutions 242 and 338 as a basis for negotiations, which called on Israel to withdraw to its 1967 borders and Jerusalem to be divided or shared between Israel and the Palestinians. I believe that a two-state solution, rooted in Resolutions 242 and 338 and using the Oslo Peace Accords as a proper framework, should be the ultimate goal of the parties.

The so-called "generous offer" that the Israelis proposed to the Palestinian negotiators at Camp David in the fall of 2000 were deeply flawed. There were a number of problems with the Israel's unwillingness to completely withdraw to its 1967 borders constitutes the most serious obstacle to peace. The Israelis have refused to fully acknowledge and recognize United including borders, road access, refugees, resources, and an agreement on the status of Jerusalem that were not adequately addressed in the Israeli proposal at Camp David. Even in its negotiations with Syria during 2000, Israel refused to withdraw completely from the Golan Heights. This is what prevented a peace agreement between Syria and Israel. The latter too will have to be considered during final status negotiations between Israelis and Palestinians leading up to recognition of a comprehensive agreement with Arab League nations.

Since 1996, both the Israeli government and the Palestinian Authority have breached provisions of the Oslo Accords. The Palestinian Authority must also accept responsibility for not being forceful enough in preventing militant Palestinian extremists from initiating terrorist attacks against Israel. The Palestinians also failed to halt propaganda against Israel in the Palestinian media, did not confiscate illegal firearms from Palestinian police and militants, and engaged in corrupt government practices under Yasir Arafat and the Fatah leadership. The Israelis, on the other hand, did not implement all of the stages of redeployment, failed to withdraw from territories that were supposed to be handed over to the Palestinians, worked to weaken the Palestinian Authority police force, and increased the amount of Israeli settlements in Palestinian territories. The first Netanyahu regime in Israel, which lasted from 1996 to 1999, further sabotaged the peace process and the Oslo Accords by expanding Israeli settlements and refusing to fully implement self-rule provisions in the Oslo Accords. This trend continued under the Barak and Sharon Administrations and now continues under the current second administration of Benjamin Netanyahu. More than two hundred and seventy new Israeli settlements have been built in the occupied territories since the beginnings of the Oslo Peace Accords.

The Palestinian Authority has proposed that international peacekeepers be sent to monitor the West Bank and Gaza Strip. The Palestinian Authority has argued that only an international observer force can bring about a real cease-fire between Israelis and Palestinians. Israel has rejected international monitors maintaining that such a peace force will restrict the movement of the Israeli military and be biased against Israel. A temporary voluntary international observer force may be necessary to help monitor a truce and make it possible to implement the provisions of the Mitchell Report, however, a lasting comprehensive peace settlement depends upon the commitment of both Israeli and Palestinian leaders to achieve peace.

A permanent peace settlement between Israelis and Palestinians must include an agreement acceptable to both sides addressing the following issues:

1. Full recognition of and security guarantees for Israel.
2. The creation of an independent and sovereign Palestinian state with its own government, police force, and secure borders.
3. The status and removal of Israeli settlements in the West Bank and East Jerusalem.
4. An agreement on the status of Jerusalem as capital city of both a Jewish and Palestinian state.
5. The return of Palestinian refugees.
6. An agreement regarding the status of Palestinian laborers working in Israel.

All of the above elements were cited in the Oslo Peace Accords. The fundamental mistake and failure of the Oslo Accords was that the agreement did not directly address solutions to these points of contention. Instead these were left to be resolved at the final status negotiations. In the meantime, vague and ambiguous wording allowed leaders on both sides to reinterpret provisions of the Oslo Accords to suit their at the moment political needs. Only when both sides set out to resolve these issues seriously can there be a lasting peace settlement.

What should be the basis for future negotiations? *Negotiating Outside The Law: Why Camp David Failed* is a scholarly book written by Raymond Hemlick, an American Jesuit priest and Professor of Conflict Resolution at Boston College. The author is very informed on all aspects of the Israeli-Palestinian conflict since he personally played a role in the early part of the peace process. I find myself in agreement with Father Hemlick's suggestion that future talks should be rooted under the auspices of international law. Professor Hemlick argues that international law should serve as the framework for negotiating a peace agreement between the Israelis and Palestinians. These include:

1. Article 2 of the United Nations Charter, which requires membership nations to renounce any territory acquired by force.
2. Security Council Resolutions 242 and 338, which requires that Israel withdraw to its June 1967 borders and relinquish control over East Jerusalem.
3. General Assembly Resolutions 181 and 194, which call for the establishment of an independent Palestinian state, the return of Palestinian refugees, and/or compensation for those unwilling or unable to return.
4. The Fourth Geneva Convention of 1949, which prohibits the settlement and colonization of occupied territories.
5. Security Council Resolution 1322, which states that the Israeli military response to the Palestinian uprising since September 2000 bas been excessive.[1]

To achieve a lasting peace, Israelis and Palestinians must implement the provisions of the Mitchell Report and acknowledge the previously-signed Oslo Peace Accords as a foundation for reaching a final and comprehensive peace settlement. Let us hope and pray that the leaders of both sides will find the courage to put aside past animosity, to develop a positive vision for the future, and lead their peoples into a new era of peace, security, economic cooperation, and co-existence based upon mutual respect for traditions, religions, and cultures.

NOTE

1. Raymond Helmick. *Negotiating Outside The Law: Why Camp David Failed* (Ann Harbor, Michigan: Pluto Press, 2004), 226.

Appendix 1

United Nations Resolutions 242 and 338 upon Which the Oslo Agreements Were Based

U.N. SECURITY COUNCIL RESOLUTION 242: NOVEMBER 22, 1967

Following the June '67, Six-Day War, the situation in the Middle East was discussed by the UN General Assembly, which referred the issue to the Security Council. After lengthy discussion, a final draft for a Security Council resolution was presented by the British Ambassador, Lord Caradon, on November 22, 1967. It was adopted on the same day.

This resolution, numbered 242, established provisions and principles which, it was hoped, would lead to a solution of the conflict. Resolution 242 was to become the cornerstone of Middle East diplomatic efforts in the coming decades.

The Security Council,

Expressing its continuing concern with the grave situation in the Middle East,

Emphasizing the inadmissibility of the acquisition of territory by war and the need to work for a just and lasting peace in which every State in the area can live in security,

Emphasizing further that all Member States in their acceptance of the Charter of the United Nations have undertaken a commitment to act in accordance with Article 2 of the Charter,

Affirms that the fulfillment of Charter principles requires the establishment of a just and lasting peace in the Middle East which should include the application of both the following principles:

- Withdrawal of Israeli armed forces from territories occupied in the recent conflict;
- Termination of all claims or states of belligerency and respect for and acknowledgement of the sovereignty, territorial integrity and political independence of every State in the area and their right to live in peace within secure and recognized boundaries free from threats or acts of force;

Affirms further the necessity

- For guaranteeing freedom of navigation through international waterways in the area;
- For achieving a just settlement of the refugee problem;
- For guaranteeing the territorial inviolability and political independence of every State in the area, through measures including the establishment of demilitarized zones;

Requests the Secretary General to designate a Special Representative to proceed to the Middle East to establish and maintain contacts with the States concerned in order to promote agreement and assist efforts to achieve a peaceful and accepted settlement in accordance with the provisions and principles in this resolution;

Requests the Secretary-General to report to the Security Council on the progress of the efforts of the Special Representative as soon as possible.

U.N. SECURITY COUNCIL RESOLUTION 338: OCTOBER 22, 1973

In the later stages of the Yom Kippur War—after Israel repulsed the Syrian attack on the Golan Heights and established a bridgehead on the Egyptian side of the Suez Canal—international efforts to stop the fighting were intensified. US Secretary of State Kissinger flew to Moscow on October 20, and, together with the Soviet Government, the US proposed a cease-fire resolution in the UN Security Council. The Council met on 21 October at the urgent request of both the US and the USSR, and by 14 votes to none, adopted the following resolution.

The Security Council,

Calls upon all parties to present fighting to cease all firing and terminate all military activity immediately, no later than 12 hours after the moment of the adoption of this decision, in the positions after the moment of the adoption of this decision, in the positions they now occupy;

Calls upon all parties concerned to start immediately after the cease-fire the implementation of Security Council Resolution 242 (1967) in all of its parts;

Decides that, immediately and concurrently with the cease-fire, negotiations start between the parties concerned under appropriate auspices aimed at establishing a just and durable peace in the Middle East.

Appendix 2

The Oslo Agreement: Declaration of Principles on Interim Self-Government Arrangements: September 13, 1993

The Government of the State of Israel and the P.L.O. team (in the Jordanian-Palestinian delegation to the Middle East Peace Conference) (the "Palestinian Delegation"), representing the Palestinian people, agree that it is time to put an end to decades of confrontation and conflict, recognize their mutual legitimate and political rights, and strive to live in peaceful coexistence and mutual dignity and security and achieve a just, lasting and comprehensive peace settlement and historic reconciliation through the agreed political process. Accordingly, the, two sides agree to the following principles:

ARTICLE I
AIM OF THE NEGOTIATIONS
The aim of the Israeli-Palestinian negotiations within the current Middle East peace process is, among other things, to establish a Palestinian Interim Self-Government Authority, the elected Council (the "Council"), for the Palestinian people in the West Bank and the Gaza Strip, for a transitional period not exceeding five years, leading to a permanent settlement based on Security Council Resolutions 242 and 338.

It is understood that the interim arrangements are an integral part of the whole peace process and that the negotiations on the permanent status will lead to the implementation of Security Council Resolutions 242 and 338.

ARTICLE II

FRAMEWORK FOR THE INTERIM PERIOD

The agreed framework for the interim period is set forth in this Declaration of Principles.

ARTICLE III

ELECTIONS

In order that the Palestinian people in the West Bank and Gaza Strip may govern themselves according to democratic principles, direct, free and general political elections will be held for the Council under agreed supervision and international observation, while the Palestinian police will ensure public order.

An agreement will be concluded on the exact mode and conditions of the elections in accordance with the protocol attached as Annex I, with the goal of holding the elections not later than nine months after the entry into force of this Declaration of Principles.

These elections will constitute a significant interim preparatory step toward the realization of the legitimate rights of the Palestinian people and their just requirements.

ARTICLE IV

JURISDICTION

Jurisdiction of the Council will cover West Bank and Gaza Strip territory, except for issues that will be negotiated in the permanent status negotiations. The two sides view the West Bank and the Gaza Strip as a single territorial unit, whose integrity will be preserved during the interim period.

ARTICLE V

TRANSITIONAL PERIOD AND PERMANENT STATUS NEGOTIATIONS

The five-year transitional period will begin upon the withdrawal from the Gaza Strip and Jericho area.

Permanent status negotiations will commence as soon as possible, but not later than the beginning of the third year of the interim period, between the Government of Israel and the Palestinian people representatives.

It is understood that these negotiations shall cover remaining issues, including: Jerusalem, refugees, settlements, security arrangements, borders, relations and cooperation with other neighbors, and other issues of common interest.

The two parties agree that the outcome of the permanent status negotiations should not be prejudiced or preempted by agreements reached for the interim period.

ARTICLE VI

PREPARATORY TRANSFER OF POWERS AND RESPONSIBILITIES

Upon the entry into force of this Declaration of Principles and the withdrawal from the Gaza Strip and the Jericho area, a transfer of authority from the Israeli military government and its Civil Administration to the authorised Palestinians for this task, as detailed herein, will commence. This transfer of authority will be of a preparatory nature until the inauguration of the Council.

Immediately after the entry into force of this Declaration of Principles and the withdrawal from the Gaza Strip and Jericho area, with the view to promoting economic development in the West Bank and Gaza Strip, authority will be transferred to the Palestinians on the following spheres: education and culture, health, social welfare, direct taxation, and tourism. The Palestinian side will commence in building the Palestinian police force, as agreed upon. Pending the inauguration of the Council, the two parties may negotiate the transfer of additional powers and responsibilities, as agreed upon.

ARTICLE VII

INTERIM AGREEMENT

The Israeli and Palestinian delegations will negotiate an agreement on the interim period (the "Interim Agreement")

The Interim Agreement shall specify, among other things, the structure of the Council, the number of its members, and the transfer of powers and responsibilities from the Israeli military government and its Civil Administration to the Council. The Interim Agreement shall also specify the Council's executive authority, legislative authority in accordance with Article IX below, and the independent Palestinian judicial organs.

The Interim Agreement shall include arrangements, to be implemented upon the inauguration of the Council, for the assumption by the Council of all of the powers and responsibilities transferred previously in accordance with Article VI above.

In order to enable the Council to promote economic growth, upon its inauguration, the Council will establish, among other things, a Palestinian Electricity Authority, a Gaza Sea Port Authority, a Palestinian Development Bank, a Palestinian Export Promotion Board, a Palestinian Environmental Authority, a Palestinian Land Authority and a Palestinian Water Administration Authority, and any other Authorities agreed upon, in accordance with the Interim Agreement that will specify their powers and responsibilities.

After the inauguration of the Council, the Civil Administration will be dissolved, and the Israeli military government will be withdrawn.

ARTICLE VIII

PUBLIC ORDER AND SECURITY

In order to guarantee public order and internal security for the Palestinians of the West Bank and the Gaza Strip, the Council will establish a strong police force, while Israel will continue to carry the responsibility for defending against external threats, as well as the responsibility for overall security of Israelis for the purpose of safeguarding their internal security and public order.

ARTICLE IX
LAWS AND MILITARY ORDERS
The Council will be empowered to legislate, in accordance with the Interim Agreement, within all authorities transferred to it.

Both parties will review jointly laws and military orders presently in force in remaining spheres.

ARTICLE X
JOINT ISRAELI-PALESTINIAN LIAISON COMMITTEE
In order to provide for a smooth implementation of this Declaration of Principles and any subsequent agreements pertaining to the interim period, upon the entry into force of this

Declaration of Principles, a Joint Israeli-Palestinian Liaison Committee will be established in order to deal with issues requiring coordination, other issues of common interest, and disputes.

ARTICLE XI
ISRAELI-PALESTINIAN COOPERATION IN ECONOMIC FIELDS
Recognizing the mutual benefit of cooperation in promoting the development of the West Bank, the Gaza Strip and Israel, upon the entry into force of this Declaration of Principles, an Israeli-Palestinian Economic Cooperation Committee will be established in order to develop and implement in a cooperative manner the programs identified in the protocols attached as Annex III and Annex IV .

ARTICLE XII
LIAISON AND COOPERATION WITH JORDAN AND EGYPT
The two parties will invite the Governments of Jordan and Egypt to participate in establishing further liaison and cooperation arrangements between the Government of Israel and the Palestinian representatives, on the one hand, and the Governments of Jordan and Egypt, on the other hand, to promote cooperation between them. These arrangements will include the constitution of a Continuing Committee that will decide by agreement on the modalities of admission of persons displaced from the West Bank and Gaza Strip in 1967, together with necessary measures to prevent disruption and

disorder. Other matters of common concern will be dealt with by this Committee.

ARTICLE XIII
REDEPLOYMENT OF ISRAELI FORCES
After the entry into force of this Declaration of Principles, and not later than the eve of elections for the Council, a redeployment of Israeli military forces in the West Bank and the Gaza Strip will take place, in addition to withdrawal of Israeli forces carried out in accordance with Article XIV.

In redeploying its military forces, Israel will be guided by the principle that its military forces should be redeployed outside populated areas.

Further redeployments to specified locations will be gradually implemented commensurate with the assumption of responsibility for public order and internal security by the Palestinian police force pursuant to Article VIII above.

ARTICLE XIV
ISRAELI WITHDRAWAL FROM THE GAZA STRIP AND JERICHO AREA
Israel will withdraw from the Gaza Strip and Jericho area, as detailed in the protocol attached as Annex II.

ARTICLE XV
RESOLUTION OF DISPUTES
Disputes arising out of the application or interpretation of this Declaration of Principles. or any subsequent agreements pertaining to the interim period, shall be resolved by negotiations through the Joint Liaison Committee to be established pursuant to Article X above.

Disputes which cannot be settled by negotiations may be resolved by a mechanism of conciliation to be agreed upon by the parties.

The parties may agree to submit to arbitration disputes relating to the interim period, which cannot be settled through conciliation. To this end, upon the agreement of both parties, the parties will establish an Arbitration Committee.

ARTICLE XVI
ISRAELI-PALESTINIAN COOPERATION CONCERNING REGIONAL PROGRAMS
Both parties view the multilateral working groups as an appropriate instrument for promoting a "Marshall Plan", the regional programs and other programs, including special programs for the West Bank and Gaza Strip, as indicated in the protocol attached as Annex IV .

ARTICLE XVII
MISCELLANEOUS PROVISIONS

This Declaration of Principles will enter into force one month after its signing.

All protocols annexed to this Declaration of Principles and Agreed Minutes pertaining thereto shall be regarded as an integral part hereof.

Done at Washington, D.C., this thirteenth day of September, 1993.
    For the Government of Israel
    For the P.L.O.

Witnessed By:
    The United States of America
    The Russian Federation

ANNEX I: PROTOCOL ON THE MODE AND CONDITIONS OF ELECTIONS

Palestinians of Jerusalem who live there will have the right to participate in the election process, according to an agreement between the two sides.

In addition, the election agreement should cover, among other things, the following issues:

the system of elections;

the mode of the agreed supervision and international observation and their personal composition; and

rules and regulations regarding election campaign, including agreed arrangements for the organizing of mass media, and the possibility of licensing a broadcasting and TV station.

The future status of displaced Palestinians who were registered on 4th June 1967 will not be prejudiced because they are unable to participate in the election process due to practical reasons.

ANNEX II: PROTOCOL ON WITHDRAWAL OF ISRAELI FORCES FROM THE GAZA STRIP AND JERICHO AREA

The two sides will conclude and sign within two months from the date of entry into force of this Declaration of Principles, an agreement on the withdrawal of Israeli military forces from the Gaza Strip and Jericho area. This agreement will include comprehensive arrangements to apply in the Gaza Strip and the Jericho area subsequent to the Israeli withdrawal.

Israel will implement an accelerated and scheduled withdrawal of Israeli military forces from the Gaza Strip and Jericho area, beginning immediately with the signing of the agreement on the Gaza Strip and Jericho area and to be completed within a period not exceeding four months after the signing of this agreement.

The above agreement will include, among other things:

Arrangements for a smooth and peaceful transfer of authority from the Israeli military government and its Civil Administration to the Palestinian representatives.

Structure, powers and responsibilities of the Palestinian authority in these areas, except: external security, settlements, Israelis, foreign relations, and other mutually agreed matters.

Arrangements for the assumption of internal security and public order by the Palestinian police force consisting of police officers recruited locally and from abroad holding Jordanian passports and Palestinian documents issued by Egypt). Those who will participate in the Palestinian police force coming from abroad should be trained as police and police officers.

A temporary international or foreign presence, as agreed upon.

Establishment of a joint Palestinian-Israeli Coordination and Cooperation Committee for mutual security purposes.

An economic development and stabilization program, including the establishment of an Emergency Fund, to encourage foreign investment, and financial and economic support. Both sides will coordinate and cooperate jointly and unilaterally with regional and international parties to support these aims.

Arrangements for a safe passage for persons and transportation between the

Gaza Strip and Jericho area.

The above agreement will include arrangements for coordination between both parties regarding passages:

Gaza-Egypt; and

Jericho-Jordan.

The offices responsible for carrying out the powers and responsibilities of the Palestinian authority under this Annex II and Article VI of the Declaration of Principles will be located in the Gaza Strip and in the Jericho area pending the inauguration of the Council.

Other than these agreed arrangements, the status of the Gaza Strip and Jericho area will continue to be an integral part of the West Bank and Gaza Strip, and will not be changed in the interim period.

ANNEX III: PROTOCOL ON ISRAELI-PALESTINIAN COOPERATION IN ECONOMIC AND DEVELOPMENT PROGRAMS

The two sides agree to establish an Israeli-Palestinian continuing Committee for Economic Cooperation, focusing, among other things, on the following:

Cooperation in the field of water, including a Water Development Program prepared by experts from both sides, which will also specify the mode of cooperation in the management of water resources in the West Bank and Gaza Strip, and will include proposals for studies and plans on water rights of each party, as well as on the equitable utilization of joint water resources for implementation in and beyond the interim period.

Cooperation in the field of electricity, including an Electricity Development Program, which will also specify the mode of cooperation for the production, maintenance, purchase and sale of electricity resources.

Cooperation in the field of energy, including an Energy Development Program, which will provide for the exploitation of oil and gas for industrial purposes, particularly in the Gaza Strip and in the Negev, and will encourage further joint exploitation of other energy resources. This Program may also provide for the construction of a Petrochemical industrial complex in the Gaza Strip and the construction of oil and gas pipelines.

Cooperation in the field of finance, including a Financial Development and Action Program for the encouragement of international investment in the West Bank and the Gaza Strip, and in Israel, as well as the establishment of a Palestinian Development Bank.

Cooperation in the field of transport and communications, including a Program, which will define guidelines for the establishment of a Gaza Sea Port Area, and will provide for the establishing of transport and communications lines to and from the West Bank and the Gaza Strip to Israel and to other countries. In addition, this Program will provide for carrying out the necessary construction of roads, railways, communications lines, etc.

Cooperation in the field of trade, including studies, and Trade Promotion Programs, which will encourage local, regional and inter-regional trade, as well as a feasibility study of creating free trade zones in the Gaza Strip and in Israel, mutual access to these zones, and cooperation in other areas related to trade and commerce.

Cooperation in the field of industry, including Industrial Development Programs, which will provide for the establishment of joint Israeli- Palestinian Industrial Research and Development Centers, will promote Palestinian-Israeli joint ventures, and provide guidelines for cooperation in the textile, food, pharmaceutical, electronics, diamonds, computer and science-based industries.

A program for cooperation in, and regulation of, labor relations and cooperation in social welfare issues.

A Human Resources Development and Cooperation Plan, providing for joint Israeli-Palestinian workshops and seminars, and for the establishment of joint vocational training centers, research institutes and data banks.

An Environmental Protection Plan, providing for joint and/or coordinated measures in this sphere.

A program for developing coordination and cooperation in the field of communication and media.

Any other programs of mutual interest.

ANNEX IV: PROTOCOL ON ISRAELI-PALESTINIAN COOPERATION CONCERNING REGIONAL DEVELOPMENT PROGRAMS

The two sides will cooperate in the context of the multilateral peace efforts in promoting a Development Program for the region, including the West Bank and the Gaza Strip, to be initiated by the G-7. The parties will request the G-7 to seek the participation in this program of other interested states, such as members of the Organisation for Economic Cooperation and Development, regional Arab states and institutions, as well as members of the private sector.

The Development Program will consist of two elements:

an Economic Development Program for the 'West Bank and the Gaza Strip.

a Regional Economic Development Program.

The Economic Development Program for the West Bank and the Gaza strip will consist of the following elements:

A Social Rehabilitation Program, including a Housing and Construction Program.

A Small and Medium Business Development Plan.

An Infrastructure Development Program (water, electricity, transportation and communications, etc.)

A Human Resources Plan.

Other programs.

The Regional Economic Development Program may consist of the following elements:

The establishment of a Middle East Development Fund, as a first step, and a Middle East Development Bank, as a second step.

The development of a joint Israeli-Palestinian-Jordanian Plan for coordinated exploitation of the Dead Sea area.

The Mediterranean Sea (Gaza) - Dead Sea Canal.

Regional Desalinization and other water development projects.

A regional plan for agricultural development, including a coordinated regional effort for the prevention of desertification.

Interconnection of electricity grids.

Regional cooperation for the transfer, distribution and industrial exploitation of gas, oil and other energy resources.

A Regional Tourism, Transportation and Telecommunications Development Plan.

Regional cooperation in other spheres.

The two sides will encourage the multilateral working groups, and will coordinate towards their success. The two parties will encourage intersessional activities, as well as pre-feasibility and feasibility studies, within the various multilateral working groups.

AGREED MINUTES TO THE DECLARATION OF PRINCIPLES ON INTERIM SELF-GOVERNMENT ARRANGEMENTS

A. GENERAL UNDERSTANDINGS AND AGREEMENTS

Any powers and responsibilities transferred to the Palestinians pursuant to the Declaration of Principles prior to the inauguration of the Council will be subject to the same principles pertaining to Article IV, as set out in these Agreed Minutes below.

B. SPECIFIC UNDERSTANDINGS AND AGREEMENTS

Article IV

It is understood that:

Jurisdiction of the Council will cover West Bank and Gaza Strip territory, except for issues that will be negotiated in the permanent status negotiations: Jerusalem, settlements, military locations, and Israelis.

The Council's jurisdiction will apply with regard to the agreed powers, responsibilities,

spheres and authorities transferred to it.

Article VI (2)

It is agreed that the transfer of authority will be as follows:

The Palestinian side will inform the Israeli side of the names of the authorised Palestinians who will assume the powers, authorities and responsibilities that will be transferred to the Palestinians according to the Declaration of Principles in the following fields: education and culture, health, social welfare, direct taxation, tourism, and any other authorities agreed upon.

It is understood that the rights and obligations of these offices will not be affected.

Each of the spheres described above will continue to enjoy existing budgetary allocations in accordance with arrangements to be mutually agreed upon. These arrangements also will provide for the necessary adjustments required in order to take into account the taxes collected by the direct taxation office.

Upon the execution of the Declaration of Principles, the Israeli and Palestinian delegations will immediately commence negotiations on a detailed plan for the transfer of authority on the above offices in accordance with the above understandings.

Article VII (2)

The Interim Agreement will also include arrangements for coordination and cooperation.

Article VII (5)

The withdrawal of the military government will not prevent Israel from exercising the powers and responsibilities not transferred to the Council.

Article VIII

It is understood that the Interim Agreement will include arrangements for cooperation and coordination between the two parties in this regard. It is also agreed that the transfer of powers and responsibilities to the Palestinian police will be accomplished in a phased manner, as agreed in the Interim Agreement.

Article X

It is agreed that, upon the entry into force of the Declaration of Principles, the Israeli and Palestinian delegations will exchange the names of the individuals designated by them as members of the Joint Israeli-Palestinian Liaison Committee.

It is further agreed that each side will have an equal number of members in the Joint Committee. The Joint Committee will reach decisions by agreement. The Joint Committee may add other technicians and experts, as necessary. The Joint Committee will decide on the frequency and place or places of its meetings.

Annex II

It is understood that, subsequent to the Israeli withdrawal, Israel will continue to be responsible for external security, and for internal security and public order of settlements and Israelis. Israeli military forces and civilians may continue to use roads freely within the Gaza Strip and the Jericho area.

Done at Washington, D.C., this thirteenth day of September, 1993.
 For the Government of Israel
 For the P.L.O.

Witnessed By:
 The United States of America
 The Russian Federation

Bibliography

BOOKS

Bennis, Phyllis *From Stones To Statehood: The Palestinian Uprising*. New York: Olive Branch Press, 1989.
Carter, Jimmy. *Palestine: Peace Not Apartheid*. New York: Simon & Schuster, 2006.
Friedman, Thomas. *From Beirut To Jerusalem*. New York: Farrar, Straus and Giroux, 1989.
Haas, Amira. *Drinking The Sea At Gaza: Days and Nights In A Land Under Seige*. New York: Owl Books, 2000.
Helmick, Raymond, *Negotiating Outside The Law: Why Camp David Failed*. Ann Arbor, Michigan: Pluto Press, 2004.
Kimmerling, Baruch. *Politicide: Ariel Sharon's War Against The Palestinians*. New York: Verso, 2003.
Miller, Anita, Jordan Miller, and Sigalit Zetouni. *Sharon: Israel's Warrior Politician*. Chicago: Academy Chicago Publishers and Olive Publishing, 2002.
Netanyahu, Benjamin. *A Durable Peace: Israel And Its Place Among The Nations*. New York: Warner Books, 2000.
Netanyahu, Benjamin. "Palestinians Should Not Have Their Own Nation," in *Israel: Opposing Viewpoints* ed. Charles Cozic. San Diego: Greenhaven Press, Inc., 1994.
Perry, Mark. *A Fire In Zion: The Israeli-Palestinian Search For Peace*. New York: William Marrow and Company, 1994.
Reinhart, Tanya. *Israel/Palestine: How To End The War of 1948*. New York: Seven Stories Press, 2002.
Said, Edward. *From Oslo To Iraq and the Road Map: Essays*. New York: Pantheon, 2004.
Said, Edward. *Peace and its Discontents: Essays on Palestine in the Middle East Peace Process*. New York: Vintage Books, 1996.
Sharon, Ariel with David Chanoff. *Warrior: The Autobiography of Ariel Sharon*. New York: Simon and Schuster, 1989.
Swisher, Clayton. *The Truth About Camp David: The Untold Story of the Collapse of The Middle East Peace Process*. New York: Nation Books, 2004.
Thomas, Baylis. *How Israel Was Won: A Concise Guide To The Arab-Israeli Conflict*. New York: Lexington Books, 1999.
Watson, Geoffrey. *The Oslo Accords: International Law and the Israeli-Palestinian Peace Agreements*. New York: Oxford University Press, 2000.

JOURNALS/PERIODICALS

Abu Sada, Mkhaimar S. "Party Identification and Political Attitudes In An Emerging Democracy: A Summary." *American Journal of Political Science* 42, no. 2 (April 1998): 712-715.

Aruri, Naseer. "The Wye Memorandum: Netanyahu's Oslo and Unreciprocal Reciprocity." *Journal of Palestine Studies* 28, no. 2 (Winter 1999): 17-28.

Cavanaugh, Kathleen. "The Cost of Peace: Assessing the Palestinian-Israeli Accords." *Middle East Report*, no. 211 (September 1999): 10-12, 15.

Danin, Robert. "A Third Way To Palestine." *Foreign Affairs*, (January/February 2011): 97.

Gavrilis, George. "The Forgotten West Bank, *Foreign Affairs*, (January/February 2006): 67.

"Groundbreaking Survey of U.S. Jews and Arabs." *The Washington Report on Middle Eastern Affairs*, (January/February 2003).

Haas, Richard. "The New Middle East," *Foreign Affairs*, (November/December 2006): 3.

Halevi, Yossi Klein. "Can The Center Hold? Understanding Israel's Pragmatic Majority." *Foreign Affairs*, (January/February 2012): 168.

Mansour, Camille. "Israeli's Colonial Impasse." *Journal of Palestine Studies* 30, no. 4 (Summer 2001): 83-87.

Roberts, Sam. "How The Middle East Got That Way," *The New York Times Upfront*, (15 January 2007): 25.

Roy, Sara. "De-development Revisited: Palestinian Economy and Society Since Oslo." *Journal of Palestine Studies* 28, no. 3 (Spring 1999): 64-82.

Sabel, Robbie. "The Oslo Accords: International Law and the Israeli-Palestinian Peace Agreements." *The American Journal of International Law* 95, no. 1 (January 2001): 248-252.

Samuels, David. "How Arafat Destroyed Palestine." *The Atlantic*, September 2005, 60-91.

Index

Abbas, Mahmoud: Hamas and, 44–45, 54; as PA leader, 29, 30, 31, 37; Palestinian elections and, 40, 41, 42; peace talks and, 72, 73; Road Map and, 51–52
Abd al-Razzaq al-Yahya, 45
Abd-Rabbo, Yasser, 52–53
Abdullah (Crown Prince), 50
Abdullah II (King of Jordan), 67
Abu Sada, Mkhaimar, 58
Annan, Kofi, 26, 32
Arab demographics. *See* Muslim Arabs (Ottoman Empire); Palestine, demographics of
Arab League, 50, 53
Arab nationalism, 7
Arab Spring, 68
Arafat, Yasir: Cairo Accords and, 15; Camp David summit and, 21–22, 23; leadership of, 29, 39–40, 60–61, 62; Mitchell Report and, 27, 37; Oslo Peace Accords and, 14, 16, 17, 60, 60–61, 61–63; PLO and, 8, 11; Tenet Plan and, 31; Wye River Accords and, 20
Aruri, Naseer H., 58–59

Balfour Declaration, 5
Barak, Ehud: defeat of, 32, 35–36; election of, 20–21; Oslo Peace Accords and, 59, 63; views of, 53, 69
Beilin, Yossi, 52

From Beirut To Jerusalem (Friedman), x, 36
Ben-Gurion, David, 6
Bennett, Phyllis, 12
Benvenisti, Meron, 12
Boucher, Richard, 32
Buchanan, Pat, 46
Bush, George W., 40, 41, 46, 50

Cairo Accords, 15, 55
Camp David summit, 21–24, 55–56, 78
Carter, Jimmy, 41, 68–69
Cavanaugh, Kathleen, 57–58
Clinton, Bill, 20, 21, 25, 30
Clinton, Hillary, 70, 71
collective punishment, 12, 23, 51

Danin, Robert, 19
Declaration of Principles (Oslo Agreement), 14, 57, 85–95
Delf, Mohammed, 45
A Durable Peace (Netanyahu), 20

Egypt, 7–8, 37
Emanuel, Rahm, 70
Erekat, Saeb, 71
European Union, 39, 40, 50

Fatah Party (PA), 29, 39; Hamas and, 13, 44–46, 72, 72–74; mismanagement by, 39–40, 40–41

Fayyad, Salam, 44–45
France, 5, 7
Friedman, Thomas L., x, 6, 8, 12, 36

Gavrilis, George, 54
Gaza Strip: Cairo Accords and, 15; demographics of, 68, 69–70; dismantling of settlements in, 36–37, 54; Egypt and, 7, 13, 37; Hamas seizure of, 44–45, 53; Intifada in, 11–12; and Israel, 8, 28, 68; Oslo Peace Accords and, 14, 16; United Nations and, 6
Geneva Initiative, 52–53
Golan Heights, 8, 27, 78
Great Britain, 5, 6, 7
Grinberg, Lev, 23

Haas, Amira, 64
Haas, Richard, 46, 67
Hagopian, Elaine C., 22
Halevi, Yossi Klein, 69
Halutz, Dan, 44
Hamas, 29, 31, 39; attack on Israel by, 42; election victory of, 40–41; Fatah and, 13, 44–46, 72, 72–74; goal/Charter of, 41, 41–42; international reaction to, 42, 45, 73; Lebanon and, 27
Hammer, Joshua, 30
Haniyeh, Ismail, 40, 41, 44–45, 45
Hemlick, Raymond, 79–80
Hezbollah, 42–44
House, E. M., 5
How Israel Was Won (Baylis), 61
Hussein (King), 20

Independent Palestine Party, 39
Indyk, Martin, 22, 74
Interim Self-Government Arrangements, Declaration of Principles on (Oslo Agreement), 14, 57, 85–95
Intifada, 9; First, 11–13, 15; Second, 23, 29
Islamic Jihad, 27, 31
Israel: current choice of, 69–70; demands of, 73; demographics of, 70; demolition of Palestinian homes by, 30, 32, 51; issues between Palestinians and, 27–32; Mitchell Report and, 26, 27; occupied territories of, 8, 11–13, 28, 68; Oslo Peace Accords and, 56–57, 58, 58–60, 61–64; Palestinian police posts and, 31, 32; Road Map and, 51, 52; settlement policy of, 27, 30, 32, 36–37, 64, 70–72, 78–79; troop withdrawals and, 59, 60; Unilateral Disengagement and, 36–38; United Nations and, 6; U.S. financial assistance to, 30; wars of, with Arabs, 7, 7–8, 8–9, 43–44; water supply and, 74
Israel/Palestine: How to End the War of 1948 (Reinhart), 63
Istanbul, 1

Jericho, 14, 15
Jerusalem: Camp David summit and, 22; Geneva Initiative and, 53; Israeli policy and, 70; Saudi peace initiative and, 53; United Nations and, 6, 28
Jewish settlements in Palestine. *See* settlements, Jewish
Jewish underground, 6, 7
Jews (Ottoman Empire), 1
Jordan, 7, 8, 11, 13

Kaddumi, Farrouk, 29
Kadima Party (Israel), 71
Karon, Tony, 72
Kennedy, John F., 67
Kimmerling, Baruch, 62–63
Kissinger, Henry, 8

Labor Party (Israel), 13
Lebanon, 8–9, 27, 42–44
Lieberman, Avigdor, 46–47
Likud Party (Israel), 13, 35–36, 68, 70

Malley, Robert, 22, 46
Mansour, Camille, 56–57
Marshall, Rachelle, 23, 44, 73
Mashaal, Khaled, 40, 45, 46
Masharawi, Sami, 42
McGirk, Tim, 70, 73
Mearsheimer, John, 67–68
Meir, Igala, 16
Miller, Anita, 64
Miller, Jordan, 64
millet system of government, 1–2
Mitchell Report, 25–27, 31
Mofaz, Shaul, 71

Muslim Arabs (Ottoman Empire), 1

Nasrallah, Hasan, 42, 43
Nasser, Gamel Abdel, 7, 8
Negotiating Outside the Law: Why Camp David Failed (Hemlick), 79–80
Netanyahu, Benjamin: as current Prime Minister, 30, 32, 37, 46, 73, 78; Oslo Peace Accords and, 19–20, 38, 62, 63, 78; settlement policy of, 70–71, 71–72
nomadic populations (Ottoman Empire), 3

Obama, Barack, 41, 46, 70, 70–71, 73, 74
Olmert, Ehud, 37, 53, 70
The Oslo Accords (Watson), 57
Oslo B Interim Agreements, 16, 55
Oslo Peace Accords: breaches of, 78–79; content of, 14–15, 15–16, 39, 77–78; Declaration of Principles of, 14, 57, 85–95; failure of, 19–24, 49, 55–56; manipulation and, 58–64; purpose of, ix, 55; results of, 49; vagueness of, 56–58, 79
From Oslo to Iraq (Said), 61
Osman I, 1
Osmanli class, 2
Ottoman Empire, 1–3

PA. *See* Palestinian Authority (PA)
Palestine: demographics of, 1, 5, 7, 28, 46, 68, 69–70; under Ottoman Empire, 1–3
Palestine Liberation Organization (PLO), 8, 9, 42, 61; Oslo Peace Accords and, 56, 57, 60, 61–62; Palestinian Authority and, 15, 16; recognition of, 11, 14, 16
Palestine National Council, 11, 12, 61
Palestinian Arab population (refugees): Abbas concessions and, 72; Camp David summit and, 21–22; demolition of homes of, 30, 32; exodus of, 7, 8, 72; Geneva Initiative and, 53; In Israeli-occupied territories, 9, 11–13, 28, 68, 69–70; Road Map and, 52
Palestinian Authority (PA): creation of, 15, 15–16; demands of, 49–50, 73; economic depression and, 30, 58; elections of, 40–41; financial assistance to, 39, 42, 73; international peacekeeping and, 31–32, 79; issues

between Israel and, 27–32; mismanagement by, 39–40, 40–41; Mitchell Report and, 25, 26, 27; Oslo Peace Accords and, 56–57, 58–60, 62–63; Road Map and, 51, 51–52; structure of, 39; Tenet Plan and, 31
Palestinian Mortgage Housing Corporation, 39
Palestinian statehood: Israelis and, 69; Oslo Peace Accords and, 55, 56, 57; Road Map and, 50, 51, 52; United Nations and, 6, 11
Parker, Jonathan, 15
peacekeeping, international, 31–32, 79
peace settlement, conditions for permanent, 79–80
peace talks: first round of, 13; post Camp David, 73. *See also* Cairo Accords; Camp David summit; Geneva Initiative; Oslo Peace Accords; Saudi peace initiative; Wye River Accords
Peres, Shimon, 13, 16, 17, 19
Perez, Martin, 47
(PLO). *See* Palestine Liberation Organization (PLO)
Popular Front for the Liberation of Palestine, 39
Powell, Colin, 27
prisoner exchanges, 42, 43

Quartet Nations, 50, 51, 54
Quartet Plan Road Map to Peace, 50, 50–52

Rabin, Yitzhak: assassination of, 16–17, 77; Oslo Peace Accords and, 13–14, 15, 16, 61–62
racism, and Zionism, 6
Rajoub, Jibril, 31
Ramon, Haim, 22
Rayah class, 2
Reform and Change Party. *See* Hamas
Reinhart, Tanya, 63
Road Map to Peace, 50–51; reaction to, 51–52
Roberts, Sam, 5
Rosenberg, M. J., 41
Roy, Sara, 58
Rudman, Warren, 25

Russia, 50

Said, Edward, 61, 62, 74
Salem, Paul, 43
Samuels, David, 60–61
Saudi peace initiative, 50, 53
Sea of Galilee, access to, 27
settlements, Jewish: dismantling of, 36–37, 54; early, 5–6, 7; expansion of, 20, 21, 23, 27, 78–79; Israeli policy on, 27, 30, 32, 36–37, 56, 70–72; Oslo Peace Accords and, 58; Road Map and, 51
Shalit, Gilad, 42, 43
Shamir, Yitzhak, 13
Sharia (Islamic Holy Law), 2
Sharon, Ariel: Camp David and, 23; election of, 24, 28, 30, 35–36; Geneva Initiative and, 53; Mitchell Report and, 27; Oslo Peace Accords and, 63, 64; Road Map and, 52; Unilateral Disengagement and, 36–38, 41
Sharon: Israel's Warrior Politician (Miller, Miller and Zetouni), 64
Shas-Party (Israel), 21
Sinai Peninsula, 7, 8
Straits of Tiran, 8
Suez Canal, nationalization of, 7
suicide bombings, 17, 23, 37
sultans, power of, 2
Syria, 8, 27

Tenet Plan, 31
Terrorism: Hezbollah and, 43; Israeli, 6, 7, 29; Mitchell Report on, 25; PA and, 31–32, 40, 78; Palestinian, 17, 19, 23, 29, 43, 55, 61, 62; PLO crack down on, 11, 14, 16; Road Map and, 50–51; Wye Memorandum and, 59
Third Way Party (PA), 39
Thomas, Baylis, 61–62
The Truth About Camp David (Swisher), 59

Unilateral Disengagement, 36–38
United Nations: condemnation of Israel by, 7; international peacekeeping and, 31–32; Palestinian states and, 6–7; Resolution 181, 11, 28; Resolution 242, 8, 11, 14–15, 16, 21, 81–82; Resolution 338, 14–15, 16, 82–83
United States: expanded settlements and, 31, 70–71, 72; Hamas and, 40, 41, 45, 46; Israel and, 30–31, 32, 46; as mediator, 30, 67, 70–71, 72, 74

Vatican, 32
Vick, Karl, 69

wars, Arab-Israeli, 7, 7–8, 8–9, 43–44
Warshal, Bruce, 37
Watson, Geoffrey, 57
Wesiglass, Dov, 37
West Bank: barrier in, 30, 37, 69; Cairo Accords and, 15; demographics of, 68, 69–70; Fatah militants in, 45; Intifada in, 11–12; and Israel, 8, 19, 20, 30, 31, 53–54; and Jordan, 7, 11, 13; Oslo Peace Accords and, 14, 16; United Nations and, 6
World Wars I and II, 3–4, 5
Wye River Accords, 20, 55, 59

Ya'alon, Moshe, 71
Yazaroorie, Ibrahim, 29
Yisrael Beytenu Party, 46
Yousef, Ahmed, 73
Yousef, Hassan, 40

Zahar, Mahmoud, 40, 45
Zakaria Fareed, 47
Zetouni, Sigalit, 64
Zionism, 6

About the Author

Dennis J. Deeb II is an adjunct Professor of History/Government at Bunker Hill Community College in Charlestown, Massachusetts and a Political Science Instructor at the University of Massachusetts Lowell in Lowell, Massachusetts. Deeb has appeared in *Who's Who In America* in 2011, 2012, and 2013. Deeb's extensive educational background includes a Bachelor of Science Degree in Criminal Justice and Political Science from the University of Massachusetts Lowell, a Masters Degree in Political Science from Suffolk University, a Masters Degree in Education Curriculum & Instruction from the University of Massachusetts Lowell, and a Masters Degree in History from Salem State University.

www.ingramcontent.com/pod-product-compliance
Lightning Source LLC
Chambersburg PA
CBHW052134300426
44116CB00010B/1891